Will the REAL Woman please stand up?

Volume One

Lessons from Rahab

By Jacqueline Peart, Inspired by the Holy Spirit

Deep Calleth Unto Deep

Will the REAL WOMEN of Destiny Please Stand Up?
Volume One
Lessons from Rahab

Copyright © Jacqueline Peart

International Standard Book Number: **ISBN 0-9533060-5-4**

Deep Publishing
PO Box 23606
London, E7 9TS
England

www.deeppublishing.com

Printed October 2006 in United Kingdom by
Athenaeum Press, Ltd, Tyne and Wear

Typesetting by Get Set Go – www.g-s-g.co.uk

Cover design by Andy Colthart – www.jharts.co.uk

Dedication

I dedicate this book first and foremost to my Father in heaven for giving me a destiny and a hope. Daddy God thank you, and do, as you will with this book so that it glorifies you!

Contents

Part Three

Will the REAL WOMEN of Destiny Please Stand Up?

Acknowledgements

To the mighty women of God in my life, my mum Normagene Peart, my two sisters, Yvonne Atkinson and Marcia Peart, I love you and am blessed continually by your dedication to the things of God. Thanks for all the proofreading, support and prayer with this book. I stand with you!

To the Deep Calleth Unto Deep Conference and Prayer team, thank you for your prayers, commitment and love. I appreciate you more than I could ever say. I stand with you all!

To my sister friends – you all know who you are because I have cried with you, laughed with you, prayed with you and grown with you. I love you, I appreciate you and I stand with you.

Apostle Ann Marie Alman. You said I'd write this book and here it is. I salute you woman of God and I stand with you!

To my leaders, Pastors Doug Williams and Anthony Hodgkinson, thank you for supporting me as I run with the vision God has given me and for not boxing me. I love and appreciate you!

To Dee Dixon Roberts, you have been my editor for years, very often without charge because you could see the vision for my life and ministry. You are a precious treasure in the body of Christ and I stand with you, I appreciate you and thank you!

Finally to every woman, every pastor, every apostle, evangelist, teacher and prophet called for such a time as this, I stand with you and acknowledge you. Together we will fulfil our destinies in Him!

Preface, Prayer and Vision

Over the years different people have asked me when I was going to write a book that wasn't poetry. Then about five years ago a prophet spoke over my life and said that I would write more than poetry books and they would be edifying, exhorting and comforting. Last year (2005) I received another prophetic word that I would write non-poetic books and the time was now. Those of you who have received a prophetic word from the Lord will know how encouraging it is. The challenge is just sometimes understanding how all that you've heard will come to pass. You pray about the word, fast in some cases and inevitably, if you're like me, you'll keep going back to it while believing and waiting for the go ahead to move from the Lord.

It's now time to move!

As you read this book my desire is that you would learn life and destiny lessons from Rahab – a prostitute whose life was transformed by the power of God when she stood up and met destiny. My desire is that you too will encounter destiny and stand up! Stand up physically, for many of you have been walking bent over for too long and sicknesses and ailments have tried to sabotage your progress. Stand up emotionally, because you have been in self-protection mode for too long. Stand up spiritually, because some of you have not been reaching up into the Holy of Holies where you can be revived, directed and empowered. Stand up mentally, for some of your minds have been sitting in familiar territories for too long, not venturing out to find new ways of doing things and being transformed! I believe that as you read and digest this book – not just reading it for information but for transformation – you will stand up in your rightful place as a real woman of destiny! As you do so you will join the millions of other women standing up in destiny, purpose and confidence!

Even now I pray for a turnaround anointing upon your life – that where you are now is not where you'll be by the time you've finished, for there will be a yoke-destroying, burden-removing anointing to turn situations around in your life for the better in Jesus name! Your life is about to turnaround! You are about to change position. Some of you have remained in the same place for too long expecting things to change. Some of you have experienced some success and so you think you have arrived. The Lord says, 'There's more for you!'

As I write I have a vision of women reaching the end of this book, lifting it up and prophetically standing up and joining with other women around the world walking in their purpose and destiny. I see women from China standing up and taking back their destinies, confidence and womanhood! I see women from Africa and the Caribbean standing and declaring they have a role, they have a destiny and identity as they teach the younger women to walk with their heads held high. Women from the United Kingdom, Ireland, Wales, England and Scotland truly becoming united to support each other as they work in unison to see God lifted up! Women from India and other parts of Asia in their traditional garments standing up and saying together, 'We are stronger, we will fulfil our destinies!' Women from the United States joyfully and expressively standing, and dancing and celebrating because where they were is not where they're going to be! Women from Eastern Europe and the Middle East slowly rising, coming out of hiding and taking a stand to pray for their families to walk in their destinies, no longer afraid, recognising that though war rages, Jesus is alive and the battle for their destiny is won in His name! I see women from South America, countries like Mexico and Brazil, laughing as they stand and recognise they have and are walking in their destinies.

The countries, the flags, the traditional dresses are too many to name, so wherever you are from, whatever country you represent, my sister, I stand with you in your destiny, in celebrating you, the real woman!

Be blessed and encouraged as you read!

Jacqueline Peart

Introduction

Welcome to *'Will the REAL WOMEN of Destiny Please Stand Up?'*
If you are familiar with any of my books in the Deep Calleth Unto
Deep series you will know that they are predominantly, poetic
inspirations, writings and thoughts. This is the first non-poetic book
that I have written.

I know firsthand what it is like not to be real and, further more, not
to know my destiny, purpose and call. I went around the same
mountains, with the same issues, living a life I had created to help
me survive. I tried to please everyone else which left me with a
fulfilment deficit. God has and is transforming me and I want to
share some of the lessons He has been teaching me with you. Near
enough every day I meet someone who is looking for their purpose,
their destiny and meaning to life. Not all of them verbalise it, but just
by the way they carry themselves, the way some of them settle for
less than their best is a tell-tale sign of someone who has not yet
captured their destiny. They are yet to find out who they are
(identity) and why they are (purpose). There is a weariness in how
they walk, they never seem to have enough energy, and sadly in
some cases they can be easily manipulated as everyone else's agenda
becomes top priority, leaving their needs lower and lower down the
list of importance.

Similarly I meet women who know their call, their purpose and their
destiny and what a difference. There is a definite way in which they
walk and talk. They don't settle, they don't compromise unwittingly,
but they move purposefully with zeal, with energy and passion. To
those standing up in the knowledge of who you are and your
destiny, I salute you and trust that this book will be one of
confirmation and comfort as you continue in your journey and
destiny.

This book has been written as a help to those yet to begin their
journey as well as a companion to those standing up in their destiny
and call. I was listening to a speaker talk about global education and
they said that it's all about training women because if you train a

woman to do something she trains others simply by teaching her children. Wow, even the world has caught onto how important it is for women to stand up in their destinies and be all God has called them to be!

For the sisters not yet standing, feeling as though you have been dealt a bad hand in life, I know you may just about have the energy to read this book, but through these pages I'm going to introduce you to a woman I have grown to admire because she, too, was dealt a bad hand. However, how she started is not how she finished. Her name is Rahab. Despite her bad start in life, her end was better than her beginning. My sister, your latter days will be greater than your former, so be encouraged – there is a light at the end of the tunnel. This matriarch is found in the lineage of our Saviour Jesus Christ. What a turn around, a prostitute and a foreigner in the lineage of the King of Kings!!! Amen!

Will the real women of destiny please stand up?

Before I began writing books I always used to skip the introduction and the preface because I wanted to get to the meat of the book and then I realized you miss something when you don't read it. The introduction gives you the author's rational for writing the book, it gives you some background/context and it can be used to encourage you as you read. So just before you get started this is a prompt for those of you that don't normally read the introduction and preface to a book – it's important – go back and read it!

Part 1 What is a REAL WOMAN of Destiny?

What is a real woman of destiny?

Webster's dictionary defines real as, *not pretend, authentic, genuine and sincere*. These are all very rich words, they are words that cannot be skated over, they need to be thought about and applied to every aspect of our lives. You see, some women can be authentic, not pretend, genuine and sincere when they're with their families; others can be when they're at work but when you are whole you are the same wherever you are and in whatever role you are playing. We can end up putting such unnecessary pressure on ourselves when we try to be different things to different people, or all things to all people.

In my early days of becoming a Christian the notion of being the same wherever I went was a challenging one. It was easier for me to adapt to the different circles I found myself in; each one expressed a part of my personality and who I was that the others didn't. It was safe. I could laugh and play my practical jokes with my family and selected friends, and I could be the businesswoman who was professional and had very clear boundaries at work. Fortunately, this didn't last.

I run a Training and Development Consultancy, **Training with Purpose**, and we offer training and development interventions and programmes to churches and organisations in areas such as management development, leadership skills, interpersonal skills, assertiveness and public speaking skills. Prior to starting this business I worked for a number of organisations as a training and development professional. It's funny how God works, He uses anything and everything to help us to grow. We just have to be available, listening and obedient.

I was to deliver a training programme, one that I had done many times before with one of my colleagues. On this occasion (this was in 1995) the session was going as planned and we were working through our programme. My colleague introduced a new exercise to the group and they began work on their individual plans. Out of the blue several of the participants began to cry as the exercise had caused them to look at personal issues. Sister, I was mad! We spoke to the women and helped them to understand what the purpose of the exercise was and how it would help them to be better managers. However, as soon as it was time for a break I called my colleague into another room for a meeting, to say I was mad is really an understatement. I wanted to know why she was making people cry! You leave your emotions outside of the workplace, you don't bring them in and you certainly don't start crying in a management development programme. Home is home, work is work, UNDERSTAND!!!! She was really surprised and asked me why I was so upset. The participants had had a breakthrough and would now not only be able to do a better job, but apply what they had learnt to their lives. For some reason the anger left me, especially after seeing how calm my colleague was and I realised that it was about me, not them or her.

So why was I so upset?

On reflection, I think it's because I couldn't hide anymore. I could always be in control of how things went. When I was at work it went like this… When I'm at home, it goes like that… When I'm in church it happens like this… Ministry is ministry and work is work, right? I realised that I was fearful of people getting to know the real me. Deep, huh? Somewhere within me I felt that if my social friends mixed with my work friends, and my work friends mixed with my church friends, somehow they would think less of me. It's amazing what the enemy will sow and if we harvest it, we reap messages that just don't make sense and, at worse, condemn us.

Eleven years on you'll be pleased to know that my whole life is ministry; there isn't all of these boxes around me, causing me to have to remember which hat to where when I'm in which situation. Jacqueline is Jacqueline all of the time. There are times when people cry in my training sessions and when I minister, there are times when I use management theories when I train and when I minister. There are even times when I cry when I'm training and when I'm ministering. The stages are different but who I am is the same. Does that mean when I go into the corporate environment I start binding and loosing, and speaking in the name of Jesus – yes it does, the difference is that it's done silently. When I'm prompted by the Spirit of God I'll share parts of my testimony and there are times when the only testimony I leave is how I behaved and dealt with the organisation.

It has been said time and time again that the only bible some people will read is your lifestyle. I have worked with organisations where I have had to ask participants if they are Christians because of the good report they have demonstrated. Then there have been times when I have not mentioned my relationship with Christ as there have been participants who try to preach the gospel at every opportune moment yet they talk about co-workers, and are always the ones late back from a tea break. They are the ones in everyone else's business, checking personal emails for long periods of time and have a dis-agreeable nature about them, telling everyone they are going to church on Sunday Authentic women, that is real women of destiny, are not duplicitous but are single-minded in their purpose to serve God and accomplish their destiny with joy and sincerity!

I know some of you are thinking, 'She's describing a superwoman.' Read my book *Inspirations for Women... A Journey to Wholeness* and you will understand that I am not describing a superwoman, but a real woman of destiny. That means she does have faults, weaknesses and fears but a real woman of destiny doesn't hide them or mask them. She offers herself up to be used nevertheless; she offers up her natural and ordinary self to the Lord and gets back supernatural and super-ordinary ability, direction and hope.

I'm trying to be real, how about you?

As you read this book and go through life begin to ask yourself whether you are real, that is:

- Are you genuine?
- Are you authentic?
- Are you sincere?
- Are you not pretend or fake?

Get reacquainted with who you are, the woman God created you to be!

In addition, as you go through life and as you read this book, ask God about your destiny, start to become aware of your destiny moments. One of the meanings of the word **'destiny'** is **'the inevitable or necessary succession of events'**. Ask God to illuminate some of the things you have gone through, like my training room experience I just described, then things will start to make more sense – you'll realise it's all been a set up.

Someone once said that God will turn your misery into your ministry, a very true statement. When I was a young Christian I remember asking a pastor: 'Why is my heart always being broken. I always seem to be in a position where someone abuses my trust, hurts me or misunderstands me'. Instead of joining my pity party, he said to me, 'Jacqui, the reason your heart is always being broken is because you are going to be used to heal the broken-hearted.' Do you know, from that moment it felt like a privilege and not a burden? What has felt like a burden in your life that God is getting ready to turn into a privilege? I believe that destiny will begin to rise up within you! I'm praying that destiny will be like a fresh fire in your belly! God's getting ready to turn your misery into your ministry!

Having this encounter helped me to make sense of why everything I write, every topic I speak or minister about, always comes back to restoration, wholeness and authenticity – being real! It's in my God-designed make up! There is something in me that has such a passion and desire to see people be real, be whole and walk in their purpose, destiny and call. In my book *Inspirations for Women... A Journey to Wholeness*, I explain some of my background. You see, I am the youngest of three daughters and being the youngest has its benefits and challenges. When you're the youngest there is a tendency for you to be spoilt by the other members of the family. I have to admit that was lovely, but the challenge in this is that when you are not being spoilt you can develop manipulative behaviours to get your own way. Even now as an adult, I am aware of these behaviours and strive to put others first!

Another challenge about being the youngest is aspiring to be like your older siblings because in your eyes, and/or sometimes in the eyes of your parents, they set the success benchmark. So if in your eyes they appear to be better or are doing better than you, you feel you need to match up and catch up. Why am I telling you all of this? Because when you feel that you are not as good as someone else, whether that is a sibling, an extended family member, another culture, gender or denomination, you can begin to develop behaviours in the hope they will enable us to fit in.

That's exactly what I did. I created a persona or mask that I believed would enable me to fit in. This has one grave downfall: you lose who you are and who you were created to be when you try to be someone you are not. It's a funny thing because even though you are accepted publicly, privately you continue to beat yourself up, put yourself down and challenge yourself to be more like the people you are trying to match up to or impress. You end up giving 'you' away and somehow losing yourself in the process. I know so many women who have woken up one morning and realised they have lost themselves in the many roles they play. In my books *'In Search of Wholeness'* and *'Inspirations for Women… A Journey to Wholeness'*, I share what I call my testimony poem, entitled, 'Looking for me'. It expresses my despair at playing the role of mother, lover, sister, friend, colleague – you name it, I was playing it. But somehow I was really just a little girl who got lost along the way! Don't worry, the poem doesn't end there. It ends with me finding 'me' in Christ!

You see, I realised in 1997, two years after becoming a Christian that I didn't actually know who I was anymore. I left the world where I was doing well by its standards and entered another world, the church world. I found that for the first two years of being saved I was simply joining another club/organisation!

In the world we danced the same dances of the time: the 'bogle' or 'water pumping' (now I know some of you are wondering, 'WHAT IS SHE TALKING ABOUT' and that's okay. They were just popular dances, something like the 'twist' when rock and roll was big in the 60's, or the thunder clap of 2000's). Everyone would be doing the same moves, went to the same clubs, parties and events at the same time, and here I was in church doing the same thing. The church folk seemed to have the same dances, the same tongues, the same shouts and all of a sudden I felt lost. I'd exchanged membership from the nightclubs and corporate UK to the church club, with us all dancing the same Holy Ghost dance, meeting at the same time each week with our yearly conference programmes and so forth.

What was different? Yes I know I was in darkness *then* and *now* I'm in the Light! But what was so different? In some ways at that time I missed being in the world (I know some people are going to pray for my deliverance right here but I have to tell the truth because I believe someone's destiny is counting on this testimony!). I missed the world because it was okay in some ways to talk about your faults, your fears and challenges over a drink and somehow you'd leave feeling better because you had the opportunity to talk over your issues. The reality of this type of pseudo co-counselling is you'd be back week after week pouring out another story over another drink, but at the time it felt comforting. Whereas, in the church, I found that no one really talked about their challenges, no one really talked about the issues they were facing unless it was testimony time or you were some famous preacher. That somehow made it acceptable because they had made it through.

It would often surprise me when I would hear a testimony from a fellow saint I sat next to, laughed with and prayed with only to realise they were going through something, yet their Sunday shouts covered the reality of their lives. Am I saying that we should all be walking around and telling everyone our woes? No, I'm not. What I am saying is that if I worship with you, if you call me your sister and you are going through something, then don't go through it alone. Choose choice people who will support you in prayer and not use your situation as a point of gossip.

Please understand that this is not a slight on any church or congregation, it is a wake up call for all of us. I know many churches have introduced Home (Cell) groups and many are working beautifully. However, even in those so often we don't get to the heart of the person and who they are. We are allowed to come and go through the motions without being challenged or without sharing the real us! Even nine years on I meet Christians who share things with me that they have never shared with anyone else because they didn't know who, how, or if anyone would really understand without judging them and isolating them. So we continue to hide our experiences, we continue to hide our true fears because every person desires to fit in and to belong.

I believe I experienced some of these challenges about being real because of the call on my life, as I said, my misery was about to become my ministry. I have found that by just telling the truth, saying when I hurt that I'm hurting, saying when I'm unsure that I'm unsure, it ministers to others because it releases them to be real and share. Let me give you an example, I remember being at a prayer meeting some years ago and for some reason every time I tried to get into prayer thoughts of fornication would come into my mind. There I was supposed to be praying for the nations and I was plagued with these thoughts that were so overwhelming that it became a distraction. After about half an hour or so, I stopped trying to pray, I stopped trying to act holy knowing that war was taking place in my mind and I said to the saints, 'I am struggling with thoughts of fornication'. Before I could think about how it would sound, what they would think of me or anything, it was out of my mouth and in the atmosphere for all to judge and/or condemn. My heart started to beat intensely as I looked at their faces. Then to my surprise one of the other women spoke up and said, 'Thank you Sister Jacqui, I thought it was just me.' Before she could finish one of the brothers then said, 'Yes, I have really been struggling in this area this week.' I was relieved! Together we prayed for each other and then we were truly able to pray for the nations, the church and whatever else the Lord had us to pray about.

On the flip side of this I know of people who went to their church with their challenges and were asked not to come back until they were serious about serving God. This approach works with some and not with others. I met one young girl who has found it hard to trust the church because of this experience and has chosen not to go back. I continue to pray that she will find her way back into the house of God recognising that in our zeal to serve God in holiness and wholeheartedness, we sometimes get it wrong! So, not everyone's experience of being real will be a positive one. Does that mean we should keep hiding? No, it doesn't. What I believe it means is that we keep forgiving, we keep believing, and we keep being real, and what you will eventually find is that others will do so, too.

I wonder how many people have been challenged by a circumstance or an issue and kept it hidden rather than getting support. I have known of children of God who attempted and/or committed suicide. That's hard to comprehend when we think of the love the Father has for each and everyone of us, yet there are individuals who with all that is available to us today cannot face their pasts, presents or futures and so cut it short. I know some of you would have gasped at the thought of a Christian committing suicide. Can I tell you something that might make you gasp again? Many of us at some point have attempted suicide, may be not physically, but spiritually, mentally and sometimes emotionally!

If I were to do a survey of how many people have at some point or the other considered ending it all, we would be surprised – thank God for His saving grace! Thank God that He is a life giver! Thank God that no matter how far down we feel we have reached, His hand is not too short to save us and help us, He continues to guide us with His righteous right hand. Suicidal actually means *'in the depth of despair, desperate and with nothing to live for'*. I have met women who after the break up with a love interest, have wanted to end it all. They have said words like, 'I'm nothing without him', 'I'll never get over this', 'Life's not worth living without him'. So they gradually give up on life, they reach the depth of despair and feel they have nothing to live for, because the past and what was has become their friend and confidante!

Sister, if this is you or someone you know, it's time to sound an alarm, it's time to sound the trumpet in your circumstance. Though your relationship may be dead, though your dreams may tarry and your thoughts of 'Will I ever?', 'Will God ever?', 'When?', and 'What if?' plagues your mind, it's time for a turnaround. If I can do it you can do it, too! I came out of doubting myself, doubting I'd be someone, wondering when God would do what He said He would and decided that I'd be a bible believing Christian, not one who selects what she reads and believes, but I would believe the whole Word! When the bible tells me I'm fearfully and wonderfully made, I am; it is settled. When the bible tells me that I am more than a conqueror; I am, it is settled! When the bible tells me I can do all things through Christ Jesus that strengthens me – I CAN!

If Rahab can do it, so can you. You have been anointed to turn around and come out of desperate situations, desperate housing projects, desperate jobs that leave you at the depth of despair every Monday morning and every Friday evening. Ministries that you thought would never come to pass for you have been in preparation and training for so long that you have begun to side with the enemy when he says, 'Did God say?' God did say and what He said He would do in your life, my sister, He will do! Destiny is waiting on you my sister! Destiny is calling you! It's time to arise, be real and stand up!

A real woman of destiny – Rahab

I know that for some, looking at the life of a prostitute may seem far from your own life experiences. That's what I originally thought until I was preparing to minister at a women's workshop and the Lord gave me the title of this book and led me to look at the life of Rahab. Her story can be found in Joshua 2:1-21, 6:21-25 and Hebrews 11:31.

Here tells the story of a real woman of destiny who was genuine, authentic, sincere, not pretend or fake!

1. *Now Joshua the son of Nun sent out two men from Acacia Grove to spy secretly, saying, 'Go view the land, especially Jericho.' So they went and came to the house of a harlot named Rahab, and lodged there.*

2. *And it was told the king of Jericho, saying, 'Behold, men have come here tonight from the children of Israel to search out the country.'*

3. *So the king of Jericho sent to Rahab, saying, 'Bring out the men who have come to you, who have entered your house, for they have come to search out all the country.'*

4. *Then the woman took the two men and hid them. So she said, 'Yes the men came to me, but I did not know where they were from.'*

5. *'And it happened as the gate was being shut, when it was dark, that the men went out. Where the men went I do not know; pursue them quickly, for you may overtake them.'*

6. *(But she had brought them up to the roof and hidden them with the stalks of flax, which she had laid in order on the roof.)*

7. *Then the men pursued them by the road to the Jordan, to the fords. And as soon as those who pursued them had gone out, they shut the gate.*

8. *Now before they lay down, she came up to them on the roof,*

9.   and said to the men: I know that the Lord has given you the land, that the terror of you has fallen on us, and that all the inhabitants of the land are fainthearted because of you.

10.   'For we have heard how the Lord dried up the water of the Red Sea for you when you came out of Egypt, and what you did to the two kings of the Amorites who were on the other side of the Jordan, Sihon and Og, whom you utterly destroyed.

11.   'And as soon as we heard these things, our hearts melted; neither did there remain any more courage in anyone because of you, for the Lord your God, He is God in heaven above and on earth beneath.

12.   'Now therefore, I beg you, swear to me by the Lord, since I have shown you kindness, that you also will show kindness to my father's house, and give me a true token.

13.   'and spare my father, my mother, my brothers, my sisters and all that they have, and deliver our lives from death.'

14.   So the men answered her, 'Our lives for yours, if none of you tell this business of ours. And it shall be, when the Lord has given us the land, that we will deal kindly and truly with you.'

15.   Then she let them down by a rope through the window, for her house was on the city wall; she dwelt on the wall.

16.   And she said to them, 'Get to the mountain, lest the pursuers meet you. Hide there three days, until the pursuers have returned. Afterward you may go your way.'

17.   So the men said to her; 'We will be blameless of this oath of yours which you have made us swear,

18.   'unless, when we come into the land, you bind this line of scarlet cord in the window through which you let us down, and unless you bring your father, your mother, your brothers, and all your father's household to your own home.

19. *'So it shall be that whoever goes outside the doors of your house into the street, his blood shall be on his own head, and we will be guiltless. And whoever is with you in the house, his blood shall be on our head if a hand is laid on him.*

20. *'And if you tell this business of ours, then we will be free from your oath which you made us swear.'*

21. *Then she said, 'According to your words, so be it.' And she sent them away and they departed. And she bound the scarlet cord in the window.*

Joshua 2: 1-21 NKJV

21. *And they utterly destroyed all that was in the city, both man and woman, young and old, ox and sheep and donkey, with the edge of the sword.*

22. *But Joshua had said to the two men who had spied out the country, 'Go into the harlot's house, and from there bring out the woman and all that she has, as you swore to her.'*

23. *And the young men who had been spies went in and brought out Rahab, her father, her mother, her brothers, and all that she had. So they brought out all her relatives and left them outside the camp of Israel.*

24. *But they burned the city and all that was in it with fire. Only the silver and gold, and the vessels bronze and iron, they put into the treasury of the house of the Lord.*

25. *And Joshua spared Rahab the harlot, her father's household, and all that she had. So she dwells in Israel to this day, because she hid messengers whom Joshua sent to spy out Jericho.*

Joshua 6: 21-25 NKJV

By faith the harlot Rahab did not perish with those who did not believe, when she had received the spies with peace.

Hebrews 11:31 NKJV

Wow! What an account, Rahab, a harlot, a prostitute, a woman of the night, someone who sold herself for money, someone who gave herself away is found in Hebrews 11 along with other men and women of faith, like Abraham, Moses, Joseph, Noah, Deborah, Gideon, David, Samuel, the list goes on. Sisters, your destiny is no longer just waiting for you, it calls you and bids you come. What was, was, it's time for the next level…

Let me share one of the definitions for prostitute from the dictionary. It is: *To sell (oneself, one's artistic or moral integrity, etc) for low or unworthy purposes.*

How many of us do not know our real value and therefore sell ourselves for a lower price than we should, or for unworthy purposes? Let me explain. Some of us are doing jobs that are below God's intended standard for us or His call for us. it wasn't where we are going, we have a destiny plan. Prostitution was just a job for Rahab, it wasn't who she was. Some of us have made our jobs who we are! So when the boss or a colleague criticises or disapproves of something we have done, we take it personally as if they are criticising or disapproving of us. You are not your job! You are not your ministry – God is the head of all!

Many people stay in jobs so long that they begin to wonder if they can do anything else. You know you are designed to be doing something else, but the locality suits you and your circumstance, you know the 'in's' and 'out's' of the job and it allows you to pursue other things. Sister, let me encourage you with something, where you are did not originally feel comfortable to you and initially you did not know the ropes. =It took time and some learning before you got the hang of the job you're doing. At the start you wondered if you would ever learn all the aspects of your role, and look at you now? It's exactly the same with any change you are going to embark upon, it looks big, it looks daunting and unmanageable but God is with you to lead and direct you. Let me share a development model with you that I use to help people understand how we learn. It's called a learning curve. There are five stages or phases. See diagram 1.

Diagram 1 – Learning Curve

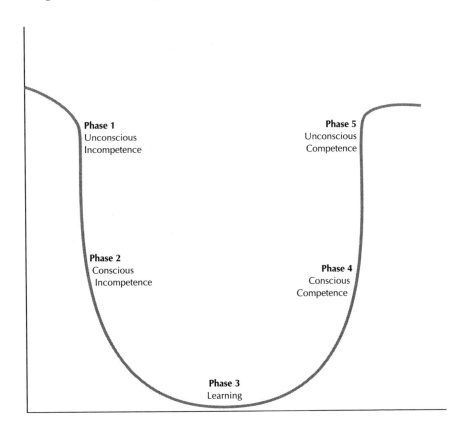

The first stage is called the 'unconscious incompetence' stage. At this first level 'we don't know what we don't know'. We are oblivious to it because it is not in our conscious mind. I remember working with a group of teen girls and I was talking to them about self-esteem and why it is important for them to have good or high esteem. It was a great session with most of them understanding the importance of feeling good about themselves and identifying the challenges they face when they don't. However, there were a couple of students who wanted to do something else. As far as they were concerned they had self-esteem and that's all good, now let's do something else. They were unconscious of their incompetence. In other words, they just didn't know what they needed to know because there was nothing in their lives thus far that made them want to know and understand about developing this crucial skill, awareness and strength.

The difference with the majority of the group was that they could all relate to a time when they didn't feel good about themselves, a time when they wished they were like someone else, and were now conscious about this fact and able to decide to do something about it.

This brings us to **Phase Two** in the learning curve – conscious incompetence. When we are conscious of our incompetence we can make an informed decision about what we are going to do about it. Some people (probably like those students who didn't want to join in) at this stage make the decision to do nothing about the area they lack skills in, and this can be the right choice. For example, if you recognise that you cannot drive a lorry, unless you need to be able to do this in life or in your job, then it's okay to make a decision to do nothing.

Alternatively, you may start a new job that requires you to do your own typing and databases, whereas in your last role you had a secretary that did this for you. You then have a decision to make about whether you don't take the job or whether you take it and go to the next phase of the learning curve and decide to learn something new.

Phase Three is where we take time to learn how to do something. It's here where we make most of our mistakes, we learn by doing and through trial and error. It's here where, if we're not careful, pride can step in as we try and work it out for ourselves instead of asking people who have been the same route to help you.

Phase Four is where you have more or less mastered the new task, role or job and you know what works and what doesn't. You do things by the book because you've just come through a learning process and you are conscious of your competence.

Finally there's the unconscious competence phase. **Phase Five** is the phase where we pick up short cuts (and, some may say, bad habits), we stop thinking about what we are doing because we are on automatic pilot. We go in to work, we drive the same route, we meet the same people, we drink out of the same mug, we answer the same queries (different people, same queries) and we just get on with it. On the rare occasion there is a problem that challenges you but on the whole you do things without thinking or unconsciously.

Let me use a generic example to expound on the phases, driving! Those of you who drive will be able to relate to the learning curve through this example. At **Phase One** you don't think about driving, it's not a conscious thought because you were either too young or were taken to where you needed to go. Then something happens to make us register the fact that we don't know how to do something. I recognised my need for driving at **Phase Two**, when I was about 19. I was standing at a night bus shelter in Trafalgar Square waiting for a bus to take me home. I had had enough. I said to my friends, 'I have to learn to drive.' I had enough of being where I was not able to go where I wanted to when I wanted to and at the beck and call of a bus.

I was ready to enter **Phase Three** of the learning stage. My mother gave my oldest sister and me some lessons, and then we both took professional driving classes. I passed first time, and I have to admit that initially I wondered if I was ever going to remember how to do everything you had to do, looking in three different mirrors, moving the gear stick, remembering when to move the clutch and how much gas to give, remembering that looking in the mirror wasn't enough as I also had to look over my shoulder in case there were any cars coming that were not visible from my mirror and, of course, there were all these other drivers on the road to be mindful of, too. It felt like lots to remember but I eventually mastered it. That's when I moved into **Phase Four** of the conscious competence stage. At this stage I did everything by the book. I manoeuvred the steering wheel with both hands as I was taught, I 'mirrored, signalled, manoeuvred', and when going to and from various destinations I noted landmarks and things of interest. I drove by the textbook.

Since then I have moved into **Phase Five**, which is the unconscious competence stage. This is where we do things naturally without thinking about them. So now, when I drive I just drive, I'm not thinking about moving the gear stick or putting my foot on the clutch or accelerator, I just drive. Because I have been driving for so long I have picked up some short cuts and very often when I get in my car to go to a familiar place, I arrive without even noticing any of the landmarks I did when I was consciously competent. If I am being driven through a familiar area, you'll often hear me say, 'I didn't know they opened up a new store there,' and nine times out of ten the store has been there for years but I have become unconsciously competent or on automatic pilot.

Why the lesson in learning curves? To help you understand that like driving, you can learn something new, if you are in a position that is below God's call for your life you can move out. Don't let the pseudo comfort of where you are keep you from growing and achieving all God has for you. I didn't think I'd do a lot of things, driving was one, writing poetry another, writing a book, standing up speaking to audiences, large and small – and enjoying it, is unheard of considering I only got one O level and a handful of poorly graded CSEs in school. How did I do it? I trusted God and continue to trust Him that what He said He will do He is going to do. I have a picture of myself when I was fifteen years old, one of those photos they take of you when you're in school. I look so sad in that picture, I was wearing unattractive glasses, sporting an uneven afro and the weight had crept on. I love looking at that picture (but I never used to).Shall I tell why I do now? Because it was me on my way to becoming who I am – a mighty woman of God! I could have stayed looking as I did, feeling as I did, and allowing fear and uncertainty to stop me from moving on.

You see, when you stay in your unconscious competence position in a job or even a ministry that God has not called you to, you miss destiny! Don't be someone who does not fulfil her ministry or purpose, allowing a lack of knowledge of who we are to keep us from truly expressing ourselves.

Back to Rahab, she was a prostitute, because of her actions. I believe she knew that title was just a title and she wasn't going to be that way always. Woman of God, the title you have been given and become known by does not have to be the title you end with. As human beings we have a habit of labelling people. Even the way we describe people in the hope that someone will remember them is often by a negative attribute. Look at Leah, she was described as the one with weak eyes or the one with lazy eyes, but it was Jacob who was the trickster. Some of us have been called by our past relationships or by a parent who didn't appear to amount to much. You'll hear words like, 'Her daddy never did become anything, poor girl.' You're not poor, you're rich in Christ Jesus. Just because your dad didn't amount to much doesn't mean you won't.

What title have you been given that no longer fits who you are or your destiny? Which titles do you need to keep and which ones do you need to say no more to? It's time for a name change. when Abraham and Israel owned their destinies their names changed. I declare in the name of Jesus that your name will be changed. Where you were known as weak you will be known as strong, where you were known as poor you will be known as rich in Jesus name!

Women of God it's time for a name change!

Part **2** Lessons for Real
Women from Rahab

Lesson 1   A real woman of destiny has the right equipment/resources

Now Joshua the son of Nun sent out two men from Acacia Grove to spy secretly, saying, 'Go view the land, especially Jericho.' So they went and came to the house of a harlot named Rahab, and lodged there.
Joshua 2:1

As we read verse one again we recognise that Rahab was a house–owner. She had the right equipment for her destiny. Had Rahab been using a hotel room or even renting someone else's accommodation she would not have known the in's and out's of the premises and/or have access to the roof or any other possible hiding place.

If she were renting, the landlord or hotelier would have wanted to know why she wanted to go up on the roof. Can you imagine her answer? 'Well, there are these two men that the King and his men are looking for, because they are suspected of being spies from Israel, here to spy out our country before utterly destroying it, except for me and my family, of course. I just have to hide them, is that okay with you?' How would the landlord or hotelier feel? Mad, because she is spinning a tale or, even worse, she is telling the truth, that she is getting ready to sell me and my people out and she wants to use my property to do it – hello!!!! Or pity for her, wondering if she had too much wine or whether her job had finally caused her to lose it, and here she is using some kind of escapism and rambling, maybe enacting the scene of some late night theatre she had watched.

Whatever the case, Rahab's destiny would have been short-circuited if she did not have the right equipment or resources and in this case it was her house! Often when prostitutes are depicted in the film industry they are either standing on a street corner wearing some kind of lewd and suggestive clothing or they are deemed as escorts for the businessman and celebrity. Either way, they are very rarely seen as house owners, or running an inn a modern day bed and breakfast or motel, unless it is a brothel.

Why do I take the time to expound on this? Because Rahab was a woman in a place that she wasn't destined for. Something in her knew that she wasn't going to be a harlot all her life, she was there trying to make a life for her family, trying to make ends meet until the waiting time was over and she was ready to meet her destiny! Deep down she knew she needed to be right where she was for such a time as this. Even where her house was positioned is significant. It was ideal for an escape route. Had she purchased a property in the middle of the city she may not have been able to hide the spies so readily.

Sister, for you to stand up in your destiny you may need a car, work for a particular company, do a particular job, be acquainted with a particular group of people, attend a certain church, or live in a certain area. But even though all the time you are living, working or fellowshipping in these areas, you know you don't belong, you know there is more for you, know there is a plan for you, a future for you, a greater hope for you. I know some people have laughed when you shared your dream, your hopes and aspirations. I know some people have been sitting and waiting to laugh at your demise! But sister, hear me loud, and hear me clear, this is not your lot, like Rahab, you are just passing through, learning the lessons that you need to learn to enable you to handle the many blessings the Lord has for you! You are not a dreamer (remember that's what they called Joseph, look how He ended up, He went from the pit, to prison, to the palace – a palace awaits you woman of God), you are not irresponsible, you are not lazy, you are not, you are not, you are not!

The plans God has for you are good, not evil, full of peace, with a future and hope! I know you have cried silently, alone and at times you have sat in church and even with so many people around you, your soul, your heart, your spirit have yearned, wept, craved, desired and hoped that God would move on your behalf. You have wondered, is this my lot? Does God care? Sister, He cares! Then why wait so long? Listen, the bible doesn't tell us how long Rahab was living on that wall in the position she was in. What the bible does say is that they knew her by name, they knew exactly where to go.

Destiny requires us to have the right equipment and resources!

1. What equipment do you need?

2. What resources do you need? For example, human resources, physical, financial, mental.

3. What equipment do you need for your journey?

Lesson 2 A real woman of destiny has a good reputation even when she's not where she should be!

Now Joshua the son of Nun sent out two men from Acacia Grove to spy secretly, saying, 'Go view the land, especially Jericho.' So they went and came to the house of a harlot named Rahab, and lodged there.
Joshua 2:1 NKJV

For the spies to have gone to Rahab means she must have been there long enough to build up a reputation, and not any kind of reputation, but a good one. Why do I say this? Because if she had a bad reputation why would someone from another country want to go and stay at her house? Rahab was also an Inn Keeper and for those of you that are like me, where I stay is very important to me. I like to stay at hotels or motels with a good reputation for not only being clean but for operating with integrity. No, I believe that while she was where she was, doing what she was doing, she made it her business to do it well!

Whatever you find yourself doing, on the way to where you're going – do it well!

On my way to arriving at this point in my life, a point where I am confident about what God has called me do, where I am assured of who I am and whose I am, I have done many different things. As a child I can remember lining up my dolls and teaching them. What I was teaching them I'm not sure, but I taught them. I remember making a little cane out of a pencil so I could point to my make believe chalkboard and making up in my mind that I wanted to be a teacher. The problem was I didn't enjoy studying and particularly studying that ended with an exam. I mentioned to you earlier how poorly I had done in my final exams in high school. I have always been an activist, a pragmatist, and that reflects my preferred learning style because I like to try things out, I like to practice new things until I get the hang of it. Over the years I developed my theorist and reflector learning styles considerably but even so, if you give me the option to try something out or read about it, nine times out of ten I'll opt to try it out for myself. One style is not necessarily better than the other; you may find that when we have certain calls on our lives, or we are in a given industry, that the way we learn will be similar. I know that for some of you these learning style terms will be new, so I have included a description of each of them in **Appendix 1.**

Anyway, back to me wanting to be a teacher. When I realised that I would have to go to university for four years, the idea swiftly left me, or so I thought! Instead, on leaving school I decided I wanted to be a chef; I wanted to go into the catering industry. I believe this is because as a child I use to spend a lot of time with my mum and she is a great cook and, like most little girls, I wanted to be like my mum (mum I know you're loving this bit, you enjoy it for truly you are a woman to be esteemed!). So catering was my second best option. I attended catering college and within a couple of months realised that I had made a dreadful mistake because I didn't enjoy the environment of an industrial kitchen. When I told my tutors, they said they had seen potential in me for management, so I was transferred to a catering management course that I passed with flying colours. After my poor exam results I was ready to work hard and turn my professional life around for the better. I left catering college with great results and eventually found my first job in catering working for British Railways' catering franchise. I started as a trainee supervisor and within a year had worked my way up to being the manager of my own unit. Within the four years I worked with the organisation I became a trainer within the company, managed the opening of one of their new outlets and had management responsibility for a number of franchises.

From there I was asked by an old manager if I wanted to run my own business doing press conference buffets and running a staff canteen for British Railways Property Board. I discussed it with my family and my mother and another friend of ours went into business and set up a company called Creole Catering (it was just a nice name, no meaning behind it for all you deep thinkers!) Again we gained a reputation for excellence and we began catering for weddings and other functions. We were doing well until a large catering company put in a bid to run the contract we had with the Railway Board, and won it. At that time I was at a crossroad because I was the person working full time in the business. I believe this was a destiny moment. I wasn't a Christian at the time and you may not be a Christian reading this book, but God loves you and He longs to commune with you on a personal basis. As I said, I wasn't a Christian then but as I look back over my life, God was and is in every part of it – the pain, the joy, the loss and the gain – He is in your life, just ask Him to show you and He will!

I remember sitting and writing down all the things I enjoy doing and all the things I hate doing. Any guesses where all my hopes pointed? To teaching! Still, the thought of the four years was too much and then the thought of being in a school five days a week was also too much, until I saw a job advert with the Post Office for a Training and Catering Executive. They wanted someone who could train in catering and manage aspects of the service. Well my name was written on the job. I got it and it was one of the most challenging jobs I'd ever done. I don't think I lasted a year, but even that was part of God's plan. I could now look for a training job because it was part of what I was doing. It's funny isn't it, the job that gave me the most pain is the one that was the doorway to all I am doing now. So the hunt for a training job began and I started work as a training officer with particular responsibility for training staff going into a new leisure centre. I worked my way up to a training and development manager across of a number of organisations and then became a training and management development consultant, which I still am to this day.

Notice something about my journey, and please note, this is just a snapshot to illustrate the fact that even when I was in the place that wasn't destined to be my final place, I was still delivering with excellence. Unbeknown to me at the time, I was building up a reputation for someone who delivers, someone who works with integrity and excellence.

Sisters, you may be in a job right now that you know is not for you, it might be leaving you depleted, de-motivated and discouraged, but I've come to encourage you and let you know again, that your end will be better than your beginning.

The job you are in now is not your final place so stop acting like it is Get happy because you're learning what you need to, to move on!

I mentioned that the job at the Post Office was one of my most challenging, but you know what, it was all part of my destiny – the **inevitable or necessary succession of events** that brought me to where I am today. Even though you are not where you should be still try to do your best. Look at Joseph, wherever he went, from slavery, to the prison to the palace he was promoted, he was put in charge until in the end he was the most important person after Potiphar.

While you are in preparation, while you are waiting for the next event or instruction from God, do your best. You don't know who is watching you. You don't know when you are going to be called. I've learned a lesson since being in ministry and it's truly that we should be ready in and out of season. There are times when I've gone to an event to hear a word and then I've been called out to share something. Similarly, I've gone to events prepared and was able to just sit and receive the word. What's the lesson? We never know when God is going to move in our lives so we need to be ready and equipped! I've heard people say when I'm called to the ministry then I'll do such and such, or when I get a new job, I'll do this and that when I move I'll make sure that this and that happens. Sisters, do it now! You don't know when God is going to be ready to move in your life and you may not have the time to do all the things you are planning, for He often moves suddenly!

As I write this book I am currently single, whole and satisfied. Have I always been? – NO!!! Read my book *Singleness* and you'll see some of the heartaches and frustrations I've gone through to get to this point. Am I always satisfied? No, but instead of letting it determine my mood, my destiny, or allowing it to linger for more than a few moments, I give it up to God, reminding Him of His promises and thanking Him for answering prayers. When I was younger in age and in the Lord, I used think. 'Oh, I want my husband to do this and do that and look like this,' whereas now, I want a man of God who knows who He is and whose he is! The things I previously wanted were material. Tiffany's jewellery, exotic holidays, stuff I have and have now done, so ladies, when my husband finds me, he finds me without the material list but a short to-the-point list. I'm no longer saying 'When I get married this, when I get married, that,' I'm fulfilling my destiny and trusting God He will bring him alongside me so we can work together in His vineyard.

What have you been putting off for when you change job, for when you are in the ministry, for when the children are older, for when…? Make a decision to do whatever you are doing now with excellence. Someone is getting ready to speak about you in high places, what is it they will be saying? She can be trusted, she is diligent, she is a woman of excellence or integrity? Or will they be saying, don't' touch her with a barge pole, she's calling herself a queen but all we see is a harlot – **someone selling oneself, one's artistic or moral integrity, for low or unworthy purposes.**

Ouch, I hear you!

Real women of destiny have a good reputation even when they are not where they should be!

1.   Do you have a good reputation? At home, church, work, within the community?

2.   What can you do to enhance your reputation? Is there someone you know that exudes the qualities you need? Don't copy them, but maybe you could let them be a role model to you.

3.   Think about who you are associated with, what's their reputation like? Is it time for an association temperature check?

Lesson 3   A real woman of destiny can be found

Proverbs 31:10 says, 'Who can find a virtuous wife? For worth is far above rubies.

A woman of destiny can be found and when she is she is likened to the virtuous wife/woman found in Proverbs, and her worth is far above rubies. Have you ever gone somewhere expecting the person to be there and they weren't? Or have you ever tried calling someone, a business call or a personal call, and all you get is the voicemail or, at worse, the number is not recognised? How frustrating! Most of us have experienced one of these at some point or the other. The person wasn't where you expected them to be. When the spies left Acacia Grove to go to spy out the land and in particular Jericho, when they arrived at Rahab's house she was found – she was there. Could you imagine if she decided to go shopping or to go hang out with a friend that day? Her destiny would have been aborted like the other people of Jericho, for they were all found utterly destroyed.

Some of you are right where you need to be to align with your destiny. You may be saying, 'I've been here long enough, in fact I've been here too long.' If that's the case maybe it's your time to meet with destiny, but whatever you do, do it in the will of God and not out of your own frustration or interpretation of what God's will is for your life.

I remember as a young girl, I think I was about twelve or thirteen years old, and my mum had told me to meet her at the Number 10 bus stop. I went to the bus stop that I thought I was supposed to meet my mum at only to find she wasn't there yet. Like the good little girl that I was (well I have to say that don't I?) I waited. I can remember buying an ice pole (for those of you not familiar with this, it's a frozen ice lolly that comes in a long tube) and leaning up against a wall proud that I was there waiting for my mum. I'm not sure how long I was waiting because I was consumed with my own thoughts when suddenly it seemed to be getting dark. I decided to run home. To my surprise my mum was there, and she was a cross between mad and glad. The atmosphere was filled with exasperation, gasps and relief because they thought something had happened to me, but the resounding conclusion was 'thank God Jacqui's home'.

I was at the wrong bus stop!

I know this is many years ago but the moral of this story remains true. When we're in the wrong place we cannot be found and not only does it frustrate our plans but it can also frustrate the plans of others. When we can't be found it takes energy from all those waiting for your gift, waiting for your anointing, waiting for your business to start, waiting for you to quit trying to be a preacher when God has called you to be an entrepreneur! Quit trying to do everything in the church and find your place so someone else can step up to the plate. So when God is moving you and directing you make sure you get clear instructions because I know you don't want to frustrate yours or any one else's destiny.

A real woman of destiny stays where she is until she gets the go ahead to move. That way, when people are sent to her she can be found! Conversely, there are those who rush, they step out prematurely and are susceptible to the wiles of the enemy. They see Susie doing it, so why can't I? Maybe it's because Susie has been in position and preparation for such a time as this. Maybe what God has for you is so specific, so unique that He needs to take more time to prepare and equip you, maybe He is still working on your reputation so that right where you are people from other countries will come to see you because they know you by name. Don't be fooled by the enemy into keeping up appearances. Don't rush because you think God is taking too long!

Look at Rahab, she remained a prostitute and an innkeeper until God said now! Right where she was she made the decision not to waste her talents or her money. So often prostitutes are synonymous with drugs, walking street corners, getting into trouble and so forth, but she knew she had to stay in that house on that wall and while she did, she made the best of it. She became a businesswoman, an innkeeper.

Positioning for your destiny is important. Have you ever wondered why it is so hard to find just the right property, in just the right area, at just the right price to buy? I believe it's because it's part of your destiny set up. All the places I have lived, I have made significant contacts, acquaintances or impact just by my presence, so even where you live is destiny-focused. That's why you can walk in and view a house and say, 'No way', and the next person can walk in and say, 'I want to put in an offer today'. Two different people, two different destinies tied up in their choices. Similarly, you can drive through an area and say, 'No way' and the next person says, 'Wonderful place to live'. Why? It's destiny! There are different spirits and principalities that operate in given areas, so we need to know where God has put us, whether it's our home, job, church or ministry.

A real woman of destiny can be found!

1. Can you be found woman of destiny?

2. Are you at the right bus stop? If you are, give God thanks and ask Him how you can ensure you stay there and know when it's time to move.

3. If you're not at the right bus stop – what are you going to do about it?

4. Who can you speak to about career planning, destiny and vision mapping?

5. What books can you read to empower you and prepare you for destiny?

6. Woman of destiny, how will you ensure you can be found?

Lesson 4 A real woman of destiny exercises wisdom

Then the woman took the two men and hid them. So she said, 'Yes the men came to me, but I did not know where they were from.' **Joshua 2:4 NKJ**

I believe Rahab exercised wisdom. Am I saying that lying is exercising wisdom? No, what I do believe is that she was not in the habit of lying because of her reputation. If she could not be trusted people would not have used her services, because I don't believe for a moment that she was the only harlot in town or more importantly the only hotelier in town. If she couldn't be trusted people would have stayed somewhere else and used other harlots, and not the ones who sell their story to the tabloid press! What Rahab did when faced with a choice of giving up her destiny and her chance to live the life she had been dreaming of, she chose to protect God's children and her destiny.

To move to our next level some of us will be faced with hard choices. We will have to make decisions that may go against our usual way of behaving to achieve a greater good. Do you know, this could be something as simple as deciding not to be intimidated by man any longer? Not to be sidetracked by friends who like where you are because they feel safe when you are the level they can reach. Destiny calls for some tough decisions! Do you remember when David feigned madness to escape Achish king of Gath whilst fleeing Saul? The bible says:

Then David arose and fled that day from before Saul, and went to Achish the king of Gath. And the servants of Achish said to him, 'Is this not David the king of the land? Did they not sing of him to one another in dances, saying;

'Saul has slain his thousands, and David his ten thousands?'

Now David took these words to heart, and was very much afraid of Achish the king of Gath. So he changed his behaviour before them, pretended madness in their hands, scratched on the doors of the gate, and let his saliva fall down on his beard.

Then Achish said to his servants, 'Look, you see the man is insane, Why have you brought him to me? Have I need of madmen, that you have brought this fellow to play the madman in my presence? **(1 Samuel 21:12-15 NKJV)**

Wow, even David had to make quick life and destiny-changing decisions that one may not necessarily agree with. If David, the one God describes as 'a man after my own heart' acted to save his life how much more Rahab.

In those moments Rahab did not act like a prostitute because she could have asked for money from the king's men or from the spies to keep quiet, or to show the king's men where the spies were hidden. She acted like a woman with a destiny agenda! Instead, she decided to hide the two men.

Real women of destiny exercise wisdom!

1. Do you exercise wisdom?

2. Do you listen to good advice or do you make it on your own?

3. Do you seek wise men and women of God when you go to make destiny decisions?

4. Do you have a spirit of discernment?

5. In all you do, do you get understanding?

6. Is there someone that exercises wisdom that can mentor you so you can draw Godly and/or business wisdom from them?

Lesson 5   Real Women of Destiny know what to hide

Then the woman took the two men and hid them. So she said, 'Yes the men came to me, but I did not know where they were from.'
Joshua 2:4 NKJV

Rahab hid the two spies from the king and his men. Hide means to keep secret, conceal and/or to cover. She knew what to hide and what to share. Many of us share things with people who are not destiny-minded and some are not even kingdom-minded! On the flipside of this some of us hide everything, we walk around carrying a whole lot of baggage, a whole load of junk that we are not meant to be carrying, and it weighs us down. Jesus took all our stuff, all our sins to the cross with Him at Calvary. We aren't meant to carry it and, furthermore, we're not wired or made to carry issues. Let me share another development model with you. This one is called Johari's Window (the window takes its name from the first names of its creators, Joseph Luft and Harry Ingham). In this context we are looking at us as human beings and what hiding the wrong things can look like.

Diagram 2 – Johari's Window

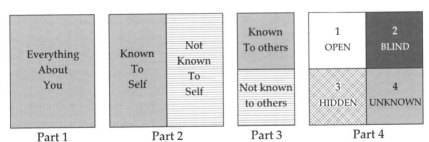

| Part 1 | Part 2 | Part 3 | Part 4 |

Imagine a frame like Diagram 2, Part 1 that contains everything there is to know about you; your likes and dislikes your goals, your secrets, your needs – everything. Of course you aren't aware of everything about yourself. Like most people, you're probably discovering new things about yourself all the time. To represent this, we can divide the frame containing everything about you into two parts; the part you know about and the part you're not aware of, as in **Diagram 2,** Part 2.

We can also divide this frame containing everything about you in another way. In this division one part represents the things about you that you keep to yourself. The other represents those parts of you that you share with other people. **Diagram 2,** Part 3 represents this view. When we impose these two divided frames one on top of the other, we have a Johari Window. By looking at Part 4 you can see *everything about you* divided into four parts.

Part 1 represents the information of which both you and others are aware. This part is your *'open* area', another term given is the *'public* area'. The type of things contained within this quadrant can be quite obvious things such as your name, your occupation, and your hair colour. Part 2 represents the *'blind* area': information of which you are unaware but others may know, particularly those who you have a relationship with, whether personal or professional. You learn about information in the blind area primarily through feedback. The type of things that we may be blind to, or are unaware of, are things like our habits, body language, mannerisms, facial expressions, even small things like the fact that you have something on your jacket that someone else sees or knows and points out to you. In my work and ministry I often give people feedback because I find that we are not always aware of how we are being perceived. A common piece of feedback I will give people in the customer service industry is to smile – a warm smile can change a new visitor's experience of an organisation or church. We can get so bogged down with tasks and duties that we forget that we are here to serve the people. Similarly, in church we can plan all these activities to attract the unsaved, yet we bombard them with 'Christianese' the minute they walk through the door. We think we're being relevant but, alas, we are sometimes blind to how we look.

Part 3 represents your hidden area; information that you know but aren't willing to reveal to others. Items in this *'hidden* area' become public primarily through self-disclosure. It's because of this quadrant why I wanted to share Johari's Window with you. I don't doubt there are some things that we need to keep hidden because it wouldn't be appropriate to share. However, there are things we have kept hidden because of our fear and embarrassment about what others will think of us, if they knew. Do you know, psychologists have found that the number one thing that keeps us hiding things is SHAME! We're ashamed of ourselves! When I first heard this it rang such a bell with me because it married with the Word, my source, guide and reference book for life and living. I was immediately reminded of Adam and Eve, how they had enjoyed a shame-free life until they ate the fruit from the tree of knowledge of good and evil and all of a sudden they were looking for things to cover their naked flesh:

> 'Then the serpent said to the woman, 'You will not surely die. For God knows that in the day you eat of it your eyes will be opened; and you will be like God 'knowing good and evil'. So when the woman saw that the tree was good for food, that it was pleasant to the eyes, and a tree desirable to make one wise, she took of its fruit and ate. She also gave to her husband with her, and he ate. Then the eyes of both of them were opened, and they knew that they were naked; and they sewed fig leaves together and made themselves coverings. And they heard the sound of the Lord God walking in the garden in the cool of the day, and Adam and his wife hid themselves from the presence of the Lord God among the trees of the garden. Then the Lord God called to Adam and said to him, 'Where are you?' So he said, 'I heard your voice in the garden, and I was afraid because I was naked; and I hid myself.'
> **Genesis 3: 4-11 NKJV**

So many of us continue to hide our shortcomings, we hide our nakedness or, in some cases, our perceived nakedness. I say again, Jesus is, was and is still the answer to anything you could have done or been through. He says, 'though your sins may be like scarlet, they shall be as white as snow.' *Isaiah 1:18 NKJV*

I can almost hear someone saying, 'It's all right for you, you don't know what I've done or where I've been?' My answer to you would be, 'You're absolutely right, I don't know and may not be able to comprehend the depth of where you have been, but sister, I still believe the Word of God, I still believe it is true. I believe it was and is inspired by God. I believe it is infallible. Other words for infallible are, 'perfect', 'water-tight', 'flawless' and 'foolproof', so when it says in 1 John 1: 9:

*If we confess our sins, He is faithful and just to forgive us
our sins and to cleanse us from all unrighteousness.*

I believe the Word!

I mentioned earlier that some of us think we have to hide some
truths about us when in fact we don't; we just carry stuff that the
enemy uses to condemn us. Let me give you an example. I told you
about how I came into training, well, although I studied and
achieved the necessary teaching certificates and training
management qualifications I never actually did a university degree!
Shock, horror!!! This used to be such a point of shame and
embarrassment for me. Anytime I was with a group of colleagues
and they would start talking about where they did their degrees or
which one they did, I would find a way to remove myself from the
conversation. In those days I made lots of cups of tea!

But God has me training at every level in public, voluntary and
private companies, and He has such a sense of humour He's put me
in situations where I train and coach university and college lecturers,
department heads, heads of schools and faculty! Isn't God amazing!
I remember one of the first times I couldn't get away to make the tea
and someone asked me the direct question, 'What degree did you do
to be doing what you're doing?' There was no escape! I took a deep
breath and swallowed hard and said, 'Actually I didn't do a degree.
I worked my way up through organisations, did the Teachers
Certificate and I'm a member of the Chartered Institute of Personnel
and Development (CIPD), and I continue to do programmes and
courses that keep me learning and relevant.' I don't think I took a
breath after my first deep intake, and I was still holding it as I waited
to see what the consensus would be after my confession. It was so
interesting. One of them repeated, 'So you don't have a degree?' I
wanted to kick her (I wasn't saved then and I did want to kick her –
but I didn't) but then I calmly said, 'No,' and before I could say
anything else someone else said, 'You know, I've hardly used
anything I learnt on my degree, tell me about the CIPD.' I did so
gladly and we ended up talking about the pros and cons of the
different types of route into professions. I didn't die, I didn't lose any
credibility, in fact I became the point of reference for the
conversation, as people said 'Well look how well Jacqui's done.

There has to be something said for vocational verses academic routes into employment.' And to think that for years I'd carried this shame and didn't have to!

Right here I feel someone's deliverance! Amen and amen! Yes sister, you can still be successful with what you've got. Am I saying don't go and study or don't do a degree? Absolutely not! I am pro education and learning, I think both qualifications and experience is necessary. What I am saying, however, is that you don't have to be ashamed of what you have in your hand. Five loaves and two fish looked embarrassing but it ended up feeding five thousand people who otherwise would not have eaten. Don't be ashamed of who you are or what you have in your hand, God can use it. Shame has kept too many women in bondage, kept us hiding, doubtful and lacking esteem. It is time to check what's in that hidden area and either get counselling, counsel or wisdom on what to do next.

Part 4 represents information that is *unknown* to both you and others. At first the unknown seems impossible to verify. After all, if neither you nor others know what it contains, how can you be sure it exists? We can deduce its existence because we are constantly discovering new things about ourselves. It is not unusual to discover, for example, that you have an unrecognised talent, strength, or weakness. Items move from the unknown area either directly into the open area when you disclose your insight or through one of the other areas first. This is the window that is full of opportunity, destiny, potential and God insight. I believe the more we find out about who we are in God the more we tap into the unknown, making it known and usable.

The relative size of each area in our personal Johari Windows changes from time to time, according to our moods, the subject we are discussing, and our relationship with different people. Despite these changes most people's overall window will look different depending on how much you hide, how much feedback you receive from others, and so forth. Someone with a very large hidden area (see **Diagram 3**) for example, depicts someone who is not very willing to share or disclose things about themselves. Someone with such a window takes few risks and may appear aloof and uncommunicative. This person may fear exposure, possibly because of not trusting others. People who fit this pattern may appear highly supportive at first. They want to hear your story and appear willing to deny themselves by remaining quiet. Then this first impression fades, and eventually you see them as distrustful and detached.

Diagram 3 – Example of a Personal Johari Window

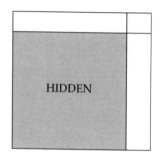

Others may have a large unknown area which would depict that they have a lot to learn about themselves. This person may be very un-self aware. You may find that other people will see this person's potential and are forever encouraging them and telling them they are good at something but they have not yet tapped into their potential, gifts and talents. They may also be focusing on what is in their hidden area so it's hard for them to see past their baggage and recognise they have a great future.

Where are you with regards to being open, real and honest? Rahab knew what to hide and when to hide it, do you? Have you become so distrustful and uncertain that you keep things hidden, believing that it's easier that way because you don't get hurt? If this book is going to transform you and your relationships and position you to be ready to stand up in your destiny and call, you're going to have to do some work! What I'd like you to do is draw your own personal Johari's Window, right here and right now. There are some blank windows **Appendix 2** for you to use – all you need is a pen. You may decide to draw several windows that represent your different relationships, for example, church, work and family and friends. Draw how open you think you are with each group, how much you think you have hidden in the different relationships, how much you are blind to and whether you need to start coveting feedback so that you can grow, and finally, how much of your potential you think you have tapped into, how much of 'you' you are yet to find out about. Ask the Holy Spirit to accompany you on this journey.

Real women of destiny know what to hide!

1.   Is there anything in your life that you are shamed of?

2.   Does this cause you to hide, fearing someone may get to know your secrets or the real you?

3.   What can you do to deal with any feelings of shame? For example, counselling, speaking with a friend, doing a course about managing negative emotions or issues of the past.

4.   What scriptures can you hold onto that will give you the peace and acceptance that you need? For example, Isaiah 43: 1-7 and Psalm 139.

5.   What will you do in the future to ensure you don't hide issues unnecessarily?

Lesson 6   Real Women of Destiny Fear God more than man

So the king of Jericho sent to Rahab, saying, 'Bring out the men who have come to you, who have entered your house, for they have come to search out all the country.'

Then the woman took the two men and hid them. So she said, 'Yes the men came to me, but I did not know where they were from.'

Joshua 2: 3-4 NKJV

A real woman of destiny fears God more than she does man. The bible says that though we are in this world we are not of this world, yet so many find it hard to serve God unswervingly because of circumstances and issues that come up. Imagine if the Queen of England, or the highest person in whatever country you are from, sent their army to you looking for someone you knew. How many of us would have feared the outcome if we didn't surrender up the person they were looking for? I wonder. Rahab was not yet acquainted with God. We know this because later verses tell us that she had heard of Him yet on the basis of what she heard it was good enough for her. She knew what man could do was only temporary but what God could do was everlasting! We cannot please all of the people all of the time, only some of the people some of the time. So if Rahab had pleased the king's men she would have been disappointing the two spies or vice versa. Sister, you cannot please all of the people all of the time because someone is bound to end up unhappy, disappointed, rejected, neglected, angry or all of the above!

That's why real women of destiny are concerned with pleasing God, not man. I have had to learn this lesson over the years and I am still learning it. My sister was asked to lead devotion/worship at her church for the first time recently. She had acted as mistress of ceremony on a number of occasions and she usually travels over to the UK from the USA (where she has lived for many years, fulfilling her destiny and preparing the way for this ministry and others) to host Deep Calleth Unto Deep events – and what an anointed, heartfelt service she delivers! But it was the first time she was leading devotion/worship in her home church. For those of you who have got ready to minister in your own church for the first time, you'll know what preparation and anticipation goes with it. So we spoke on the phone and we prayed for God's will to be done in all things and I shared this one thing that I have learnt in my short life in ministry: Do everything unto God! Set your face as flint and do everything unto His glory and for His approval. You see, over the years I have sought approval from someone for one thing or another. If it was not a partner's approval of how I looked in my dress or looks compared to another, it was a boss for approval of my work; if it was not the boss it was my family, if it was not my family it was my friends and if not my friends, then the audiences at my training or speaking engagements, and if not them, then my leaders and pastors. You know, the funny thing is a hundred people could tell me how great I was, how anointed I am and what a blessing I was to them, yet if the one person I desired the approval from didn't say anything, I didn't or couldn't hear the hundred!

Sister, God has approved of you. There is no one on this earth dead or alive that can approve of you and accept you more than or like the Beloved can – no one. The more I craved the approval of others the more it would somehow slip away from me and, at worse, someone else would appear to be getting the accolades I so desperately desired. Then one day I realised that until I truly approved of myself, until I truly accepted me, how could I expect others to? Finally, it's as if God gave me the secret to serving Him (it's no secret really because it's littered throughout His Word). It was just that at this time I was ready to hear it, and it is this: put Him first, make Him the person I want to please, make Him the one I desire approval of and then everything else will be added to my life. Just seek Him first. It removes such unnecessary weight; more of that baggage in the hidden quadrant of Johari's Window is removed. And it's true, put Him first. The funny thing is that all of those people whose approval you long for sometimes will never 'get you', but now it's okay as your success or feelings are not dependant upon their reactions. In addition God will use some of those same people at different times, and often when you don't think you need it or when you least expect it they will come along side you and encourage you. It's then that you receive it as a welcome surprise and encouragement, not a void filer. Let me give you an example. In 2005 I was launching one of my books, **Inspirations for Women...A Journey to Wholeness**, at a venue in London. As always I had told my pastors what I was doing and they continued to support my vision.

Before I carry on it's important for us to recognise that our leaders are men and women who daily work at their call to shepherd you. Does this mean they'll miss it sometimes? Yes, it does, but does it mean that they don't care or are immune to getting hurt? No, it doesn't, because as your leader or pastor they have extra responsibility for not only themselves and their families, but for a congregation. Why do I say this? Because even as I write I sense that there are some of you reading this who have sought approval from your leaders and you have not received it in the way that you had expected or hoped. You feel sidelined and at worse, ignored and rejected. Sister, let me encourage you to speak with your leaders if this is the case. It may not always be your pastor you get to speak to but one of the elders or a responsible Cell group leader. Please do not let the enemy chase you from your destiny and into the arms of a new church that God has not ordained, because not only will you be in the wrong place but you will carry feelings of resentment or lack of care into your new church. (It's a bit like if you have ever had a bad break up with a friend or boyfriend and you are not healed. You then begin to look for the same fault with your new friend or partner and, worse still, you shut down your emotions in the hope that you will protect yourself.) God has a way of finding us when we run away. Be encouraged, it doesn't necessarily mean that where you are is not where you should be, but if you are sensing a destiny move, then do it right. Pray, seek counsel from your pastor, get his release and leave in love. Always be able to go back to a church you left with joy. I know some people have experienced spiritual abuse where they have felt the church had used them and in some cases misused and abused them. If it is a bible-believing, Spirit-led, Jesus-declaring church, ask God to help you find a way to forgive them so it is no longer a place you look at with hurt and bitterness but with understanding and peace. Only God can tell you if you should go back, but there's nothing like having peace when you move on. **Bitterness kills!**

Now to the example I was going to share. As I said my leaders knew of and supported the launch but like most local pastors with a community and global assignment, they are not able to attend everything that happens within a thriving church. It would be physically impossible! They were unable to attend the launch and that was fine with me particularly as my senior leader, Doug Williams, had attended previous Deep Calleth Unto Deep events, spoken at several of them and has a close eye on me and my ministry. (Thanks Pastor D, I know your heart for me and this ministry and I appreciate it and you. Pastor, I celebrate you and what God is doing in your life and the life of our church family, Emmanuel Christian Centre in Walthamstow.) God is good!

The evening of the launch came and we were putting the final touches on the hall when I looked up and saw one of my other leaders, Pastor Anthony. I was so blessed to see him, I nearly knocked him over with my hug. He had worked his weekend out so that he could attend a number of functions and the launch was one of them. I'm not sure he will ever really know what that did for me, when I wasn't looking for approval or acceptance but just to serve God and be approved by Him, He sends one of His shepherds or angels. Sister, when you stop looking to please man and just to please God, He will send you what you need when you least expect it. I believe Pastor Anthony thought he was just coming to support me, but he did much more than that just by his presence. It was an amazing blessing to me; I truly believe he was there to represent Daddy God in the flesh. He even said some life and ministry affirming things on the night that I thank him for, but above all it was his simple presence when I least expected it that was a blessing. Thank you.

As I just finished writing that last sentence my heart went out to our young people. If you are a parent reading this book, there is a lesson there in what took place. No matter how much you support your children in words, with the provision of clothing, food, school and love – they also need your presence. God knows why we need to be in His presence because we receive direction; we receive guidance, love, intimacy, understanding, approval, acceptance, hope, the list just goes on and on... In all that you do in terms of practical tasks for your children, never forget the power of your presence!

Proverbs 1:7 says *'the fear of the Lord is the beginning of knowledge.'* Fear Him and you've begun to acquire real knowledge and understanding!

Sister, I know that many of you reading this can relate to what I'm saying. So many of us have made decisions to please others and later regretted because of the damage done. I sometimes speak with young women who are not yet out of school already pleasing man – usually a boy who is not yet a man – purely because he approved of her, told her what she wanted to hear, told her that she was beautiful, that she was different to all the other girls, she was going somewhere, how she was the only one for him, until he got what he wanted, then all of a sudden the decision she made to please this boy left her feeling used, unwanted and at worse violated. Some become pregnant and still haven't left school yet – if you're a young woman reading this book and have found yourself in this situation, you are not alone. The bible says:

> He knows about everyone, everywhere. Everything about us is
> bare and wide open to the all-seeing eyes of our living God;
> nothing can be hidden from Him to whom we must explain all
> we have done. But Jesus the son of God is our great high
> priest who has gone to heaven itself to help us; therefore let us
> never stop trusting him. This high priest of ours understands
> our weaknesses, since he had the same temptations we have,
> though he never once gave way to them and sinned.
> **Hebrews 4: 13-15 TLB**

Jesus understands your weaknesses. He experienced them and yet listen to what the scripture says, He has gone to heaven itself to help you. Cry out to Him; ask Him to forgive you and to teach you how to be all that He has created you to be. Daughter, you are still beautiful, so walk with your head high. Daughter you are special and unique and your destiny is not yet aborted, you are indeed on schedule, you have been called for such a time as this. Don't let a couple of mess-ups detour your greatness – for you are fearfully and wonderfully made. That same scripture goes on to say that you can go boldly into the throne room of grace. It says boldly, you don't have to go sheepishly, but with your head up walking with the authority of a princess in Him:

> So let us come boldly to the very throne of God and stay there to
> receive mercy and to find grace to help us in our times of need.
> **Hebrews 4: 16 TLB**

Real women of destiny fear God more than man!

1. Why do you fear men more than God?

2. What can you do to build up your confidence in God so you fear (reverence) Him more than man?

3. What will it take for you to understand that you have been accepted by the beloved and no man or woman can accept you like the Father?

Lesson 7   A real woman of destiny is not intimidated

> *So the king of Jericho sent to Rahab, saying, 'Bring out the men who have come to you, who have entered your house, for they have come to search out all the country.'*
>
> *Then the woman took the two men and hid them. So she said, 'Yes the men came to me, but I did not know where they were from.'*
> **Joshua 2: 3-4 NKJV**

By Rahab pleasing God more than she did man she demonstrated that she was not easily intimidated. Intimidation means to be **threatened, bullied, fearful, coerced** and **terrorised**. Intimidation is a spirit and a strategy that the enemy uses. This is often the reason why we please man rather than God, because the spirit of intimidation threatens and coerces you to stay where you are or to please man. Intimidation has such a negative effect on the recipient because it can almost leave you in a cold sweat after an encounter with it. Once again we see Rahab stand up to the king's establishment without missing a beat, without fear, and without being bullied into giving up the spies.

I believe Rahab had met her fair share of bullies in her time, how could she not have given her profession? She had met many a man that had tried to intimidate her, coerce her into doing favours for them, even tried to threaten her into doing things. God knew all of this. It was part of her destiny plan. When David remained in the fields alone, defending his life and his sheep's against the wildlife, it appeared at first look to be just a job. However, David was learning how to fight, learning warring skills as he killed bear after bear and lion after lion. So when it was time for one of his destiny moments – the fight against Goliath, he was well prepared for Goliath's growls and intimidation tactics – they didn't faze him; Goliath was just another bear or lion and, more to the point, David was prepared!

Rahab had dealt with men that used intimidation tactics for years and so at this crucial destiny moment, she did not let fear hinder her, she was not going to be intimidated by the king's men. She was ready for her destiny moment! Even though Rahab's job was to please men – when it really mattered she chose to please God! She went against everything her profession was renowned for, listen to what the writer of Proverbs says about prostitutes:

> For the lips of a prostitute are as sweet as honey, and smooth flattery is her stock in trade. But afterwards only a bitter conscience is left to you, sharp as a double-edged sword. She leads you down to death and hell. For she does not know the path to life. She staggers down a crooked trail, and doesn't even realise where it leads.
> **Proverbs 5: 3-6 TLB**

Rahab was an exception to the rule she did know the path to life. I hope as you read this book you don' think I'm trying to make Rahab out to be some martyr, after all surely there are some more apt women of destiny in the bible that we could learn lessons from. Yes there are other women of destiny in the bible, many of which I have spoken about when ministering, and no, I'm not trying to make her out to be a martyr even though in her own way I think she was. What I'm trying to be is real. Each time I mention that Rahab was a prostitute, I'm not depicting her job, I'm depicting what it meant because I know right now in and outside of the body of Christ there are men and women who **'sell (oneself, one's artistic or moral integrity) for low or unworthy purposes'**. She's real to me because even though I have never been a prostitute in the job sense, in the definition of the word I too have sold my artistic integrity for lower than it is worth. For example, I know that in my work as a consultant, when it was time for a price increase I didn't want to put up my prices because I didn't' want to appear greedy, yet the value of what I was delivering was far more than my fee. We have all at some point sold our gifts, integrity, services and so forth for less than they are worth.

Rahab to me signifies what so many mothers do; they give up on themselves until the children are grown and they make sacrifices to raise their children and prepare for their families. I have this image of Rahab servicing customer after customer while thinking, 'Okay, this one puts food on the table for another week,', 'Okay, this one helps to buy dad's medication,' and 'This is for when we get out of here because this is not where we belong', or 'This is not who I am but just what I do and I'm coming out'. So you work extra shifts, two and three jobs as you care for your family! I know I've said it several times already but I'm going to say it again. Rahab is more like many of us than we may have initially perceived. I believe she was a woman caught in a bad situation on her way out! She was there long enough to walk into her most life-changing destiny moment.

Sister, you're where you are for such a time as this. No matter how bad your situation may seem, there is a destiny moment that is getting ready to call you out of that situation. It's time to go to a new level of faith – no longer accepting where you are as your 'lot' – your situation will not intimidate you! Even now I pray for an anointing of boldness to flow over you, that you might shake off intimidation, shake off the weights that so easily beset you and get ready to stand up – your destiny calls!

Real women of destiny are not intimidated!

1. Who have you allowed to intimidate you?

2. Why have you allowed them to intimidate you?

3. How can you develop boldness?

4. Who can support you?

5. Who can tell you about courses, books and seminars you can attend to develop your assertiveness skills?

6. Will you say no more to intimidation today, in the name of Jesus?

Lesson 8   Real women of destiny are bold

Then the woman took the two men and hid them. So she said, 'Yes the men came to me, but I did not know where they were from. "And it happened as the gate was being shut, when it was dark, that the men went out. Where the men went I do not know; pursue them quickly, for you may overtake them.'
Joshua 2: 4-5 NKJV

Another word for bold is confident – to stand up in and achieve our destinies we must be bold! I have not always had the boldness that I have now. God has done and continues to do a marvellous work. As a child I was chatty, full of jokes and fun at home and with a very selected few but on the whole I was very quiet, shy and lacked confidence. When it was time for me to go to catering college, I had taken off some weight and was looking nearly as stunning as I do now! So because I was in the background in school, never part of the popular cliques, it was time to change so I created a pseudo confidence that was my mask to protect my insecurities and uncertainties. I was louder than I had been previously and was able to get away with things that others were not. This worked for me and I became the popular girl everyone knew. This carried over into my social life and though it was great something was missing. That something was Christ. It was in 1995 when I gave my life to the Lord, when I realised that this personality I had developed was to mask my loneliness and low self-esteem. In 1997 when I prayed a simple prayer, 'Lord, make whole, make me who you created me to be', it was then that the Lord showed me all the strategies and manmade interventions I used to present this confident image. Over the years He has and is still chipping away at my masks and showing me that I am strong in the power of His might, I am the child of the King so I can walk boldly. He has given me authority to trample on serpents and scorpions, and over all the power of the enemy, and nothing by any means shall hurt me. (Luke 10:19) I started to receive real boldness and confidence that can only come from a right relationship with the Father.

So sister, if you have found yourself being intimidated by man, if you have found yourself lacking the confidence to do the things and make the decisions you know you ought, be encouraged, God is still on the throne. He is still in the making-over business. Tell me something, what stops you from moving on? Fear I hear someone say. Didn't God say that He has not given you a spirit of fear, but of power and of love and of a sound mind? (2 Timothy 1:7) If you want to come out of your double-mindedness, fear, coercion and intimidation you need to start to live the Word. Not just having a happy routine devotional time, I mean reading, believing and living the Word. It will change your life forever for the better! Don't get me wrong, the attacks will still come, doubt will still knock and at times, like Rahab, your heart will be beating fast but you will stand confidently and give an answer to those who require it.

A real woman of destiny is bold!

1. Why do you lack boldness/confidence?

2. Who told you that what you had to say wasn't important?

3. What will you do to take back your confidence and boldness?

4. How will you start?

5. Who will you start with?

6. When you have said yes in the past when you should have said no, why did you? What did you fear would happen?

7. Do you want your confidence back, in other words do you want to be made well?

Lesson 9   Real women of destiny go the extra mile

Then the woman took the two men and hid them. So she said, 'Yes the men came to me, but I did not know where they were from. And it happened as the gate was being shut, when it was dark, that the men went out. Where the men went I do not know; pursue them quickly, for you may overtake them.'
Joshua 2: 4-5 NKJV

Real women of destiny go the extra mile to fulfil their destiny. They limit their story and their issues and give that little bit extra. You see, Rahab could have just told the king's men that the spies had come to her house and left, but she didn't, she went on to say that when it was dark they left and if the king's men pursue them quickly they might overtake them.

Rahab took the time to explain the set up and then to give clear directions and instructions. Have you ever been lost and had to stop and ask for directions? I know on many occasions, especially before the wonderful invention of satellite navigators, when my map had failed me I'd have to pull over, wind down my window and ask a passer-by for directions. I know that in the current climate we live in that we have to be cautious about who we stop and ask as well as who we stop to listen to, but there is something about those times when you are lost or when you are not sure where you're going and you need good instructions or directions. Sometimes I've been faced with people who pretend they haven't heard you calling out to them; they put their heads down and just kept walking. Then you have those who give you vague directions like, 'You've missed it love, it's back there'! Back *where* you wonder. Rather than prolong the discussion I've kindly thanked them and ventured back *there*. There are the ones who tell you where to go by using all the names of roads, roundabouts and motorways that you have never heard of or taken the time to notice. Every so often you get that one person who is clear, helpful and goes the extra mile with you.

Destiny requires us to do that bit extra, go that bit further. I remember putting air in my tyres at a local petrol station when a woman came over to me and asked for directions to the Blackwall Tunnel, which links east and south London, somewhere I know well. I tried to give her the most simple and direct route but I could see she was nervous about getting lost and she had her two children in the car with her. In the end I said I would drive to the road that would lead her straight to the tunnel. All she had to do was follow me to a certain point – she was over the moon, someone was taking the time out to help her get to her destination.

Rahab took the time out to get the king's men away from her destiny and to another destination, but she didn't just send them away she went the extra mile to ensure the spies' safety.

> *And she said to them, 'Get to the mountain, lest the pursuers meet you. Hide there three days, until the pursuers have returned. Afterward you may go your way.'*
> **Joshua 2: 16**

Rahab's going the extra mile wasn't a one-off thing, because later when it was time to send the spies on their way she gave good instructions. Again she could have quite easily just said, 'You can go now, you'll be safe,' but she didn't. She told them how long to wait, where to go – she went the extra mile!

Let me take a moment to pause and ask you three questions.

1. **Do you go the extra mile?** Whether at work, church or at home – this at first might seem to require a simple 'yes' or 'no' answer. The reality is some of us will find that we go the extra mile at home because we are with our loved ones who we care about and have chosen to be with, so we work harder there, look after it, sow into it. Whereas when it comes to work – we may only give or do what is expected, not thinking about going the extra mile. As the bible says, if we only love those who love us, what reward do we have? Do not even the tax collectors to the same? (Matthew 5:46 NKJV) If we only go the extra mile at home but not at work we are missing a biblical truth.

2.   **What can you do to go the extra mile to help usher in your destiny?** For some of you this might be something as simple as making the calls to those people who you keep saying you're going to call, but never do! One of those people could be the key to your destiny. For others it might be something as simple as taking time out to learn something new, rather than just getting by with the knowledge you have for your journey. Going the extra mile could be making time to learn more about where you believe God is taking you. I heard a story once where a young man went to his pastor and said he was led to go on the mission field to Africa. The pastor was happy for the young man as he had just finished bible school and was full of zeal and passion to do the things of God. So his pastor said, 'That's great. What part of Africa are you called to?' The young man was naïve and said, 'All of it.' The preacher went on to explain how big Africa is and that he needed to seek God as to which part he was to go to first. The pastor then asked the young man, 'What's their main trade?' The young man paused, as he wasn't sure, so the pastor said, 'Okay, do you know what their main challenges are?' The young man regained a little of his confidence and said, 'Yes, poverty.' The pastor then asked, 'Do you know how many Christians are already there or what their main religion is?' The young man didn't know, but he thought he would give an answer and said, 'There are some Christians already there.'. (Help!!!) Finally, the pastor asked, 'What Christian agencies are already operating there that he might consider working with?' The young man once full of passion and zeal realised that his passion and zeal would take him so far and sustain him but he also needed more than that to get him there; he hadn't done his homework! The pastor's job was done; he had helped the young man get prepared for his destiny simply by asking him some fundamental questions that would enable him to go the extra mile to fulfil his call. He didn't discourage him, he just simply asked him the right questions to stir him and prepare him to go in the right direction.

Where and what has God called you to? What courses, seminars and books can you find to help you prepare? Too often I meet people who somehow think that one day everything is going to be alright. I admire their faith but the bible says, 'Faith without works is dead.' (James 2:26) We need action! I mentioned earlier that wholeness is at the centre of my call and so if you look at my library of books you will find that a lot of them heavily lean to that topic, as well as books about leadership and healing. I go the extra mile to ensure I am prepared for what God has called me to. Do you?

3. **If you have gone the extra mile, how did it make you feel?** The reason I ask this question is because sometimes the enemy can make us feel as though we don't have the time to make that call or that we can only do what we can do, God will understand. The devil can even cause us to think that it doesn't pay to go the extra mile. He'll quickly remind you of the time you helped someone out and how they repaid you with lies, hurt or a lack of gratitude, or nobody else is going the extra mile so why should you? Listen sister, it pays to go the extra mile. Christ went the extra mile when He went to Calvary, but He didn't stop there. He went into hell and took back the keys to death! What an example we follow. We may not always see the fruit of the things we do but I can assure you God sees them and what you do in secret He will reward you publicly for. So think back to times when you went the extra mile and instead of buying into what the enemy wants you to believe, remember how blessed you felt!

One last thing about this lesson, it costs you – you see, going the extra mile costs. It could have cost Rahab her life and the life of the spies but she stepped out nevertheless, and look at what she received for that stepping out – her name in the hall of faith (Hebrews 11) and a place in the lineage of Christ!!

Stepping out costs but is it worth it? – I believe it is!

Real women of destiny go the extra mile!

1. Do you go the extra mile?

2. What areas do you go the extra mile in?

3. What stops you from going the extra mile?

4. What will you do or sacrifice to go the extra mile? For example, watching less television, committing to go out to midweek services or making time for someone else.

Lesson 10 – There is order in the life a real woman of destiny

(But she had brought them up to the roof and hidden them with the stalks of flax, which she had laid in order on the roof.)
Joshua 2: 6 NKJV

Real women of destiny have their life in order. The bible says that Rahab took the spies up to the roof and hid them with stalks of flax, which she had laid in order on the roof. As I read this verse the word 'order' just jumped out at me and I believe the Lord illuminated this word so that His daughters of destiny would put their houses in order, ready for their destiny.

Sisters, this is a wake up call! Get your house in order! What you have been putting off, put it off no longer; what you have been saying, you will do when you've got time – the time is now! Don't be like the five foolish virgins that were caught with no oil in their lamps because they were unprepared when the Bridegroom came (Matthew 25 1-13). Sisters, don't be caught sleeping or with your house in disarray – it's time to get your life in order!

There are four different areas where real women of destiny should ensure there is order. **The first area is in our relationships.**

Do you know Jesus Christ as your Lord and Saviour? If not this is the first relationship that you need to get right, because without Him everything, including your relationships, will be temporary – having Jesus in your life brings eternity and hope! (Go to page 128 and accept His invitation to join God's family).

If you are a Christian are you right in your relationship with the Father? Are you still connected to Him or have you grown complacent and distant? Do you hear Him when He calls to you or do you have to wait until your Sunday service to hear what Father God is saying to you through your pastor or guest speaker? Tell me, do you sense His heart beat on situations that need prayer? Do you sense His tears when tragedy hits the earth? Do perceive His move in the earth before it happens or when it's come and gone? Tell me, do you tarry in His presence just to muse with Him, reason with Him, listen to Him, worship Him, be intimate with Him? Tell me, is your relationship with the Father in order?

Sister, despite what lies you may have been told, I'm here to set the record straight. When you confess your sins, God is faithful and just to forgive you and cleanse you from all unrighteousness. (1 John 1: 9) Do you hear what God is saying? He is the same today, yesterday and forever so His word doesn't change. That means He is still faithful, He is still just and He will still forgive you of **all** unrighteousness! Not some unrighteousness, but **all** unrighteousness! **All** means, the entire, complete, every single one, and every bit – there is no distinction or hierarchy of the things He will forgive, He forgives it **all**. Romans 8: 31-39 (TLB) says:

> *What can we ever say to such wonderful things as these? If God is on our side, who can be against us? Since He did not spare even His own son for us but gave Him up for us all, won't He also surely give us everything else? Who dares accuse us whom God has chosen for His own? Will God? No! He is the one who has forgiven us and given us a right standing with Himself. Who then will condemn us? Will Christ? No! For He is the one who died for us and came to life again for us and is sitting at the place of highest honour next to God, pleading for us there in heaven. Who then can ever keep Christ's love from us? When we have trouble or calamity, when we are hunted down or destroyed, is it because He doesn't love us anymore? And if we are hungry or penniless, or in danger, or threatened with death, has God deserted us? No, for the scriptures tell that for his sake we must be ready to face death at every moment of the day – we are like sheep awaiting slaughter.*

> *But despite all this, overwhelming victory is ours through Christ who loved us enough to die for us. For I am convinced that nothing can ever separate us from His love. Death can't, and life can't. The angels won't, and all the powers of hell itself cannot keep God's love away from our fears for today, our worries about tomorrow, or where we are – high above the sky, or in the deepest ocean – nothing will ever be able to separate us from the love of God demonstrated by our Lord Jesus Christ when He died for us.*

Sisters, like the apostle Paul, who was inspired by God to write these words, I am convinced that nothing can ever separate us from His love! So if you know that you have not been where you ought to be in relationship with God it's time to get in order, for the Father bids you come!

How's your relationship with your family and friends, are they all in order? Are there any issues that are outstanding that need to be discussed or resolved? What's your relationship like with your mother and father? I know there are people who have never known their fathers, or their mothers for that matter – this in itself will present certain challenges whether we are conscious of this fact or not. Let me share an example of this with you. I was asked to review a manuscript by a powerful young man and as I reviewed it, I noticed that he had talked much about the pros and cons of his relationship with his mother and step father, but there was only a very small reference to his biological father where he recounted a fun moment. When I mentioned this to him, initially he didn't see any challenges with it but as we spoke about how his absence could have impacted him, he began to share some of the things he would have wanted his dad to know. Sometimes it's just a question that will prompt us to think about things that are hidden or blind to us (remember the two areas in the Johari's Window?) This will open us up to learning more about ourselves, understanding our relationships and getting healing, if necessary, from the Lord about any unresolved issues.

So if there are any relationships that you need to work out, do so with God. This will ensure you don't overlook them or make up for them through your children, go into denial or put pressure on your existing relationships. Have you resolved childhood hurts and pains or is indifference and self-protection your portion? If Christ were to come back now – would you have any regrets? Would there be any relationships that you wished you had repaired, started or even cut off? Sisters, it's time to get our relationships in order.

What about your relationships with your church family? Are they in order? You know, there is something about relationships in church. When they work and God is in the centre of them they are beautiful friendships that cannot be compared. However, when they don't work they can be so painful because we believe that because we are in Christ that it will be different and, if we're honest, some of us think they should be perfect. So when we are hurt by our brethren it can leave us disappointed and damaged. Is there anyone in church you need to forgive? Is there anyone who has hurt you, overlooked you or even rejected you? Sisters, it's time to get our relationships in order!

The **second area** in our lives that we need to get in order is our work affairs. As mentioned before, some of us find it difficult to go the extra mile at work. However, the reality is that some people find it difficult just to do their fair share. It's as if the world owes them something. Sister, no matter what you feel your job has done to you, what you feel they owe you – it's time to get your work affairs in order. Clean up! Clean up your computer and take all your personal material off of it and put it on discs or a memory stick. Check that you are meeting all the required standards expected of you. Instead of treating appraisals and performance reviews as a pain or necessary evil, start seeing them as opportunities to grow, to receive feedback, so that you can move with more ease into your destiny. What could you be doing differently at work that will bring more order? What training programmes does your employer offer that can assist you, for example, time management and project management programmes? What systems can you introduce to help yourself – some of you may need to invest in a personal digital system that helps you keep appointments, reminds you of things to do and so on. Or you can just learn to utilise your existing computer programmes, diary and mobile phone. Some of you would be surprised to know how many things your mobile phone does besides making and receiving calls!

For those of you in business – does your company's legal structure help you grow or does it restrict you? Have you got the right branding and marketing for the audience you are trying to attract? Are your taxes and books up to date and kept safely ready for audit at anytime? Do you employ the right staff or are they just people who were available? Are you aware of grants and funding that is available to help you develop your business? Those of you who have been talking about or thinking about starting a business, the time is now! God is getting ready to transfer wealth into the body of Christ, are you ready? Sisters, it's time to get your work and business affairs in order!

The **third area** that we need to ensure is in order is our ministry affairs and church business. Are you where you are supposed to be within the body of Christ? Is the church you attend the church that is local to you and is it the one where your gifts and talents are used? Is it a church that celebrates you or tolerates you? Is it where God would have you for this season? Does your church share the vision that God has put on your life or is it just a comfortable place to be? Are you walking in your purpose and destiny or are you just getting happy every Sunday? Do you know your ministry? Sister, it's time to get your house in order – destiny calls you!!

The **fourth area** that we need to get in order is the area of our finances. This includes your ability to spend wisely, invest and how you live your life per se.

Matthew 6: 21 says, *'For where your treasure is, there your heart will be also.'* Where is your heart?

I did a word search in a bible dictionary and found the following facts:

- Nearly 50 per cent of the parables in the bible mention money (16 out of 40)
- The King James Bible mentions gold 417 times, silver 320 times and money, which is mentioned 140 times – which totals **877** references
- This is in comparison to 'faith', mentioned 247 times, 'believe' mentioned 143 times and 'hope' mentioned 129 times – which totals **519** times

Money is mentioned 358 more times than faith, hope and believe. That tells me that God has important things to say about wealth.

More now than ever people use money as a bolster for their lack. We use it to bribe, for security, for power, to impress and keep up with others, to help our confidence, to prove a point, to be accepted, for comfort and to help our self-esteem. None of these, I believe, were God's original intention for its use. God is the only one that can give us the acceptance we desire, the esteem and confidence we lack – money cannot do it. Women can end up spending money when they don't' have it or don't need to. Why? Somehow we link it to our self-esteem and worth. Let me give you some more research about compulsive spending and our esteem.

Research by Hanley and Wilhelm (1992) found:

- Compulsive spenders have lower self-esteem than normal and a poor relationship with money.
- Compulsive spenders believe money enhances their self-esteem – money makes them feel better.
- Compulsive spenders have the idea that money can solve all their problems.
- Compulsive spenders never have enough money to meet their needs.

Sisters, if you are a compulsive spender and your heart is tied to your money it's time to get your finances and life in order. Some women don't know how much they owe. There are women who do not open letters that come in a brown envelope because it will be a bill, yet they continue to spend. They continue to keep up appearances and a lifestyle that they are not yet ready for. I believe God has the best for us; we are joint heirs to the throne, so tell me, how often do you see a princess or a prince begging? Not very often! So we are intended to have money, indeed the bible says that it is God that gives us the ability to get wealth (Deuteronomy 8: 18)

For those of you who God has given wealth, it is not just so that you can drive a nice car and live in a big house, even though that's great, it's so that you can be a blessing to the body of Christ. There are some people who have wealth and all they do with it is hide it, they are so scared of spending the money they have hoarded that in the end it doesn't benefit them or anyone else. I believe these people have an issue with security. They worry, 'What if I don't have any savings and such and such happens?' I understand that. I think it is wise to have savings put away for a rainy day and in preparation for your children's children. However, if it could be helping the things of God then think about sowing something. The bible is clear in the story of the talents that He will repay us with more if we make it work for others, and for those of us that just sit on it, even what we have will be taken away. (Matthew 25: 13 – 30).

Matthew 6:24 says, *'No one can serve two masters; for either he will hate the one and love the other. Or else he will be loyal to the one and despise the other. You cannot serve God and mammon (riches).'*

If you are reading this and know that you have used money for things that only God can provide, it's time to repent, seek professional advice where you need to concerning your finance and get your finances in order!

Here are ten tips that can help you to manage your money and get out of debt.

Tip One – Repent and receive forgiveness
Repent for poor money management and for having an unhealthy relationship with money and ask God to work with you as you endeavour to transform and renew your mind.

Tip Two – Decision Making
Make a decision to make a change! Everything starts with a decision, in this case you're making a decision to put your finances in order and choose God in all things.

Tip Three – Work it out
Sit down and work out exactly how much you have, owe and who you owe it to. You may decide to use a spreadsheet, computer package or good old-fashioned pen and paper. Whichever you choose to use have a clear idea of where you stand financially.

Tip Four – Budget
Be realistic and work out what you can afford to repay and still stay within your budget. Remembering that your TITHE IS ALWAYS A MUST. That's 10 per cent of your earnings brought into the church! I know that when people get into debt or are struggling financially tithe is an easy option to leave out. It's not. There are testimonies upon testimonies of people whose finances turned around the minute they started tithing again. For me more than anything it's a matter of obedience!

Tip Five – Be disciplined
Don't borrow any more money or take on any more debts until you have repaid what you already owe. In the UK at least several times a week you will hear how debt it spiralling – with 1 in 4 people in debt. One of the things that keep people in debt, or should I say bondage, is credit cards. Buy now, pay later. It sounds good and is often good for that moment until the bills come with the interest

piled on. Sisters, it's time to get our finances in order!

Tip Six – Watch your daily spending

If we just take out money as and when we need it from the ATMs we don't quite know how much we are spending. If you want to get your finances in order take a set amount of money out of the bank at the beginning of the week and stick with it. No unnecessary purchases.

Tip Seven – Organise your bills

Try and pay all your bills, including utility bills, by direct debit. You will find that most suppliers offer you a discount if you do this.

Tip Eight – Switch your suppliers

Check in newspapers or on the internet for who is offering the best deals for the following:

- Gas and electricity
- Mortgage
- Insurance policies, for your car or house, for example
- Savings accounts
- Bank accounts

Once upon a time no one really changed their bank accounts or mortgages, who you signed up with is who you stayed with. Not so anymore. You can choose who you bank with and for how long. Some banks offer better rates than others so utilise this to get out of and stay out of debt!

Tip Nine – Get a cheaper credit card and cut up store cards

Try different providers and you'll probably be able to find a credit card with a better rate than you're paying now – particularly for transferred balances. Most debt counsellors will tell you to cut up your store cards unless you are very disciplined and able to pay them off before the interest kicks in. If you're not disciplined then cut them up as the interest rates are normally much higher than normal.

Tip Ten – Sow and confess the word!!!

Sowing prospers you. I remember back in the nineties at a point when my business was quiet I sat in a large convention listening to the speaker asking for an offering. I sat there thinking I can't afford to give anything right now but I continued to listen and remain open to the Holy Spirit. The speaker was saying we ought to sow like we've never sown before because God was getting ready to honour us. I felt the Holy Spirit nudging me and I was trying to ignore the leading because I thought, 'I can't, I just don't have it right now, it would be irresponsible of me to spend any money right now.' In the end I chose to obey and gave the largest offering I had ever given up until that point. I trembled through writing the cheque and finally placed it in the offering bucket. This was the Saturday. On the Monday, I received a telephone call asking me to do a piece of work. As I put the phone down I received another call and it was more offer of work. God more than outdid Himself with that one act of obedience to sow. Sister, I know it's hard when you're not sure how you will manage, but again I believe the word, for it says, 'He has never seen the righteous forsaken nor his seed begging bread'.(Psalm 37: 25) God is honourable. Choose not to let your own tongue curse you or keep you in poverty or lack by constantly saying, 'I'll never have money because... Everything's too expensive, I can't afford it...' or 'I never have any money at the end of the month'. What you say is what you will have. Sisters, it's time to get our finances in order and begin to the live the truth, let the poor say they are rich; when we don't have enough, He is more than enough! Use the Ten Tips to come out of the bondage of debt and lack. Your destiny is counting on it!

Sister, right now let's pray. 'In the name of Jesus, I pray that you will be released from every generational curse, every word that has been spoken over you to keep you where you are. Every demon assigned to my sister's finances to hold her back from receiving the ability to get wealth we bind in Jesus name, for the bible says that we have been given the keys to heaven and whatever we bind on earth, will be bound in heaven, and whatever we loose on earth will be loosed in heaven. We loose freedom in the name of Jesus, we loose prosperity, clarity and increase in the mighty name of Jesus! Amen.'

Sister, you are rich in Him, you are prosperous in Christ Jesus! It's time to side with God about your finances and not with the enemy! Get ready because as you apply wisdom, knowledge and understanding to your situation God will turn your finances around for the better!

A real woman of destiny has her life in order!

1. Are you serious about your life being in order? Then go back and read this lesson again and take action!

Lesson 11 Real Women of Destiny understand timing (seasons)

Now before they lay down, she came up to them on the roof,
Joshua 2: 8

The bible says that before the spies lay down for the night, Rahab went up to see them on the roof. A real woman of destiny understands timing (her season) and she went before they lay down. How many times do we miss the boat because we got up late, got the wrong date on our calendars, or our timing and sensitivity to a situation was out? I often pray that I would be like the sons of Isachaar who the bible says had an understanding of the times, to know what Israel ought to do (1 Chronicles 12: 32). Rahab understood the times. She went just before the spies lay down and ultimately received the response she had hoped for.

This reminds me of when my sisters and I were young. We had a strategy for getting what we needed, whether it was ice cream or a 'yes' to a request from my mum. We would ask her just before she fell asleep! You see, we would interpret her groans and/or her weariness as a 'yes'. I don't remember how long this tactic worked but it was the right time for us to get what we wanted or needed. She was in a position where it was difficult to say no, and that's what Rahab did. She had protected them and they were probably weary as well as thankful at this point, so just as they were about to lie down, she stepped in to get what she needed.

It's important for us to understand the times and seasons in our lives. You see, there are times when God gives us a season of rest yet we try to busy ourselves, asking Him to give us something to do or change our circumstance. There are seasons He has given us to be active for Him, serving Him and accomplishing His purpose, yet all the way through we're looking to rest. We need to understand our season. King Solomon describes this well when He said:

There is a right time for everything,
A time to be born,
A time to die;
A time to plant;
A time to harvest;
A time to kill;
A time to heal;
A time to destroy;
A time to rebuild;
A time to cry;
A time to laugh;
A time to grieve;
A time to dance;
A time for scattering stones;
A time for gathering stones;
A time to hug;
A time not to hug;
A time to find;
A time to lose;
A time for keeping;
A time for throwing away;
A time to tear;
A time to repair;
A time to be quiet;
A time to speak up;
A time for loving;
A time for hating;
A time for war;
A time for peace.
Ecclesiastes 3: 1-9 TLB

Sisters, we need to pray that we understand the times and our season so that we will know what we ought to do, when! You see, there are different definitions for seasons and timings, two of them are as follows:

Kairos – is a Greek word that means, *the right time, opportune time, season, proper time and appointed time*. This is God's timing, we have no control over this. This type of season is when God moves and steps in. A common way of describing this type of timing is His divine timing or due season.

The second type of timings is **Chronos** – this refers to the order of things, it is here we get the word chronological from. It means *sequential and in order*, for example, Monday follows Tuesday, 1.00 am follows 12.00am, June comes after May; it is the order of things.

If you are like me there will have been times when you have wanted things to happen today or now but it was a kairos or a God-thing was what we needed. If I look at this in relation to marriage, some of you reading this book have been watching the biological clock, or the calendar clock, looking at your age and the time it's taking to get married. But God looks at the kairos, His clock, His due season and His appointed time for you. Sisters, my encouragement to you is don't rush and settle for His 'permissive' will when He has a 'perfect' will for you. When Abraham had Ishmael, God permitted that to happen but it was not His perfect will, Isaac was.

What have you been waiting on to happen? What have you been praying about and hoping for that seems to be taking forever? The Lord says, 'Stop looking at chronos and start to expect my kairos, and when I move it will be over and above what you have been hoping for. I will do such a new thing for you and in you that people will marvel.' God says, hold on, He has not forgotten you, though the vision tarry, wait for it, for it shall surely come!

Real women of destiny understand timing (seasons)!

1.   What season are you in?

2.   What season is your family in?

3.   What season is your church in?

4.   What season is your work or business in?

5.   How will you keep check of what season you are in?

6.   What can you do to prepare for the different seasons in your life, emotionally, physically, mentally and spiritually?

Lesson 12   Real women of Destiny Go up Higher

Now before they lay down, she came up to them on the roof,
Joshua 2: 8

Real women of destiny know that they have to come up higher to receive, they can't stay where they are and shout up. They have to go up into the presence of the Lord. They go up higher in praise, in worship and in prayer...

Rahab could have waited for the spies to come down in the morning or shouted up to them with her requests but she knew that the time was now if she and her household were to be saved, and that she would have to go up to a higher place for it. Sisters, some of us have stayed far away from the Lord and shouted requests, hollered demands, calling it prayer and wondered why a response was long in coming. God desires us to come up higher. Higher in praise, higher in worship higher in our relationship with the Father!

I was in the states in 1999 when God began to do something new in my life. How it manifested was through me feeling uncomfortable. I was busy hollering to the Lord, shouting up to Him that I want more of Him, asking Him to speak to me! But I just didn't feel any connection, I couldn't sense God's presence and so I began to feel more and more distant and frustrated. I began reading the Word to see if I could see what God was saying to me or doing in my life at the time – nothing! It was Sunday morning and time to go to church and I prayed that God would speak to me through the worship or the message – nothing! So by the time we arrived back at my sister's house I was tired, dejected, frustrated and hurt – I wanted God! My sister and I didn't exchange any words. I just went and sat on the bed and I was now mad. How comes God says that we should call to Him and He will answer and show me great and mighty things that I do not know (Jeremiah 33:3) I said, 'God I've been calling, where are you?'

For those of you that think I'm verging on blasphemy – capture my heart, I love the Lord with all that I am, with all that I can be, with all that I will ever be and He knows that. I just have a real Father-daughter relationship with Him – one where I'm real, about my emotions, my motives and fears.

Anyway, the tears just began to roll down my face as I waited to hear, and then He gave me a vision of me in my living room, shouting upstairs to Him and Him humbly standing next to me waiting for me to stop shouting so that I could hear Him say, 'I'm right here daughter, where I've always been.' My immediate thought was, so why didn't you just answer me, but before that thought had time to land, I sensed the Lord say, 'I didn't' want to startle you because I was closer than you thought.' He had me, like He always does and always will. It was me that had moved into a downstairs room shouting up instead of just going up higher in Him. I felt so refreshed in that moment, so loved, so accepted, so looked after and cared for, it made me realise why I serve Him. It was in that moment that I understood why people die for the gospel. In those moments from deep within me I realised that if I die, I die, but I just have to serve Him because of my immense love for Him. Even then, as I had the thought, 'I said to the Lord, you don't really want me to die for you do you?' He said, 'Yes, to your flesh'. In those moments in September 1999 I got it, I've got to come up higher. I praised, worshipped and then was led to write the following poetic inspiration – be encouraged as you read:

I'VE JUST GOT TO SERVE HIM

I've just got to serve Him
I don't know what else to say
I don't know how else to describe it,
But I need to let somebody know that amidst my trials and
tribulations, my uncertainties and doubts I've just got to serve Him
For He's my King, my Lord, Jehovah, my Saviour Jesus Christ
You see there's no other before Him, none other after Him
So I've just got to serve Him!

I tell you the truth brothers and sisters, friends and who knows, even
some enemies
That I've got to serve the King of Kings, the Alpha and Omega, for
He's my Beginning and He is my End.

I've just got to serve, Adoni, El Shaddi, my Almighty God,
For He is the All-Sufficient One; He is God all by Himself; He doesn't
need anybody or anything else!
You see, He is Omnipotent, Omnipresent, Omniscient is He.
You see He's been my Rock, my fortress and my very present help
He's been my comforter, my healer, my restorer and repairer
He's been my friend, when I was friendless, my hope when I had none
He's supported me, encouraged me, and yes, rebuked me as well.

But when I weigh up the odds and I estimate the cost
When I balance the pros and balance the cons, the 'fors' and the
'againsts'
With Him on my side things always come out better
So, I've just got to serve Him.

I don't always understand Him
I don't always immediately agree with Him; sometimes it takes time,
some reasoning and some processing for me to see the plans He has
But no matter what,
No matter the cost
I've just got to serve Him.
I can't do it half-heartedly
I can't hang around outside the veil
Flirting in the Holy Place
Settling for the anointing
It's the Holies of Holies or it doesn't make any sense
It's time for the glory of the Lord to manifest in this land
I've come this far, in fact, too far to play religious games
I've got to be intimate
I've got to hear Him for myself
I've got to meet Him whatever the cost
I have had and have the gifts and they are truly wonderful
I've had and have the blessings and they'll continue to flow
I've had and have the teaching; the preaching as well and I know
there's more in store
I've ministered and been ministered to, that my friends will
continue.

But can you hear the desperation
Can you sense my neediness amidst the words and the syllables of
this precious prose I write?

You see, I've just got to have the Giver,
The One who blesses and not just the blessings,
The original Teacher and Preacher needs to be in my heart and in my
mind, and in my soul and in all that I am, and in all that I can be.

You see I've just got to serve Him!

If I die, I'll die
If I'm to be broken then I'll be broken
Please listen very carefully for it's taken me nearly five years to say
I'll truly die for the gospel
I'd always hoped that it was someone else's calling,
Someone else's appointment
So when I say nothing else matters please believe that I've reached a
place in my relationship where nothing else matters
Because I've just got to serve Him!

My Prince of Peace, my strength, my courage and my source
I love the Lord with all my heart and all my mind and I will seek
Him early while He may be found.
Friends, if you don't know Him
If you've never been introduced to Him
Never spent quality time with Him
Please don't let this day go pass
Without inviting Him to spend some time with you.
I guarantee you,; you won't want Him to go
I know some have left you after promises made but
He'll never leave you nor forsake you
He'll stay as long as you want, as long as you make Him welcome
He's a God who loves and cares for you
A God who sent His only son just for you and me,
That you might have a new life.

And if you've become a lukewarm Christian
One who comes and goes and is satisfied with a weekend affair

Think about His goodness, and what He has done for you
Your soul ought to cry out Hallelujah and thank Him for saving you.

To go beyond the veil takes courage,
Courage only He can give to you
So if you're bored with mediocre
Fed up of being in the comfort zone
And your desire is to go for more
Press in and on, forgetting those things that are behind.

This poem is just a reminder that He desires more from us

Whatever your level, whatever your status, you can always push in further!

You see WE JUST HAVE TO SERVE HIM,
But, ONLY IN SPIRIT AND TRUTH!

Real women of destiny go up higher!

1. What can you do to go up higher? Higher in praise, higher in worship, higher in relationship and intimacy with the Lord

2. What stops you from entering the presence of God? For example, distractions of the day, self consciousness, timidity, other people's opinions and perceptions

3. What will you do push past any hindrances that stop you?

4. He bids you come – will you?

Lesson 13   Real women of destiny know what the Lord has done

And said to the men: I know that the Lord has given you the land, that the terror of you has fallen on us, and that all the inhabitants of the land are fainthearted because of you.
Joshua 2: 9

Rahab said 'I know that the Lord has given you the land' – real women of destiny know what the Lord has done and what He is doing. How do we know what the Lord is doing? We listen to what the Spirit of the Lord is saying. Earlier we talked about how important it was to go the extra mile and a part of that was about gaining knowledge. It strengthens our faith when we see what God has done for others because we then know it is possible for Him to do it for us. That's why real women of destiny know the Word; they endeavour to understand what God has done in the lives of the patriarchs and matriarchs so they can gain wisdom and understanding for their destinies.

For us to learn effectively we also need to be good listeners because we can often gain much knowledge from listening to others', to sermons, seminar speakers, tapes and so forth. The challenge for us as women is learning how to listen effectively. Many of us have probably never thought about what type of listener we are, yet this is important in helping us to develop and understand ourselves. Below is a list of types of listener, which one best describes you?

The Empathetic Listener – Someone who gives you time and space and is able to make you feel at ease while you are speaking. They will say things like, 'I understand what you're saying', 'I have experienced that too'. They have a way of making you feel at ease with yourself and your experiences.

The Impatient Listener – Someone who can't wait for you to hurry up and finish what you are saying. They may speak at a pace and have a poor attention span. This listener will also finish your sentences and interrupt you mid flow of your conversation.

The Preoccupied Listener – Someone who appears to not want to be there. Even while you speak they may be fidgeting with things, writing, doodling or even continuing to work on the computer, use machinery or on the phone. An example of this may be the shop assistant who says, 'Can I help you?' while still engaged in a personal conversation on the phone or with a fellow colleague.

The Inquisitive Listener – Someone who helps you to say more than you thought you would say, because they ask you relevant and probing questions that make you have to think about what you are saying. They may ask questions like, 'How did that make you feel?', 'How did that sound to you?', 'Can you picture a different scenario or how you could have got a different outcome?'

The Proud Listener – Someone who already thinks they know what you are going to say so they don't really have to listen to you. This listener will even correct you about what you have said about your own experience! They believe their opinion is more important than you or yours.

The Timid Listener – Someone who doesn't feel they are important so they don't challenge or listen actively because they don't expect to be involved in the conversation or decisions. Often this listener will not make eye contact with you.

Active Listener – Someone who exercises effective and appropriate body language, and verbal and non-verbal communication like eye contact, smiles, nods and leaning slightly forward to demonstrate how engaged they are. They will also paraphrase, clarify and summarise what the speaker says appropriately.

Now you have had the opportunity to review the different types of listener I'm sure you can identify with all of them because you have probably been all at one point or another. The assignment for a real woman of destiny is to be an active, inquisitive and empathetic listener more often than she is the other types. How well do you listen? How well do you study to gain knowledge? Woman of destiny, it's time to acquire the knowledge that you need to take you to your next destiny moment – Rahab had the knowledge she needed, she knew what the Lord was doing. What do you need to know? Who do you need to listen to? Who have you become an impatient or a proud listener with that may have the key to your destiny?

Real women of destiny know what the Lord is doing!

1.   Do you?

Lesson 14 Real women of destiny are not hard hearted

'And as soon as we heard these things, our hearts melted;
neither did there remain any more courage in anyone because
of you, for the Lord your God, He is God in heaven above and
on earth beneath.
Joshua 2: 11

Rahab said 'Our hearts melted'. Real women of destiny are not hard-hearted; they allow their hearts to melt, another word for soften. I meet women everyday who have allowed their hearts to be hardened because of issues, hurt and pains of the past. They protect their hearts so much so that it's difficult for them to show their feelings. I remember sharing this fact at a workshop I was facilitating and one of the participants said, 'But doesn't the bible tell you to guard your heart?' *(Proverbs 4: 23)*. I responded by telling her she was quite right, the bible does say that we ought to guard our hearts, the problem is that so many have barricaded their hearts in behind layer upon layer of self-protection mechanisms, put a padlock on it, iron and steel bars and a few more safety locks for good measure! They can't get out and no one can get in! No matter how many times we get hurt or wounded, we need to forgive, receive healing and move on. I know that may sound challenging to some of you reading this and we will deal with the steps to becoming real and leaving the past behind in Volume Two. It is possible, not always easy, but possible.

Before becoming a Christian I dated a young man who I believed I loved at that time, before I really knew what real love is. I hoped that he would be the one that I would marry, have children with and live happily ever after. During that relationship for one reason or another I had cried many a tear, some justified and some not as I allowed my imagination and lack of esteem to get the best of me. The relationship came to an end and something in me just said, 'That's it, no more tears. I'll never cry over another man again as long as I live', or words to that effect. And I didn't, I hardened my heart, acted as if was okay and carried on with life. When God called me and I finally answered, I could not believe the tears I cried, I was one of those you see at the altar every Sunday weeping – God was softening my heart again. Now, anyone who knows me, knows I cry, unashamedly, I weep. Why am I telling you this? Because I believe someone reading this book right now has come out of a relationship and, like me way back then, is saying, 'That's it, no more' and are getting ready to lock up their heart. Sister, the bible says that a broken and contrite heart, He will not despise (Psalm 51: 17). So you may feel broken, betrayed and hurt right now but this too shall pass! Weeping may endure for a night but joy comes in the morning (Psalm 30:5). I know from first hand experience that you can never be real when your priority is not getting hurt or self-protection. God can be trusted!

I have mentioned self-protection several times throughout this book and I want to explain what I mean. Different people will use a variety of strategies to evade being hurt or from being real. Some become defensive so you never get too close to them; others never take anything seriously because it keeps everyone at arms length; others just work and work and work; and others withdraw, you hardly see them and when you do they are very much into themselves. All of these strategies are manmade and like the fig leaves Adam and Eve sewed together when they realised they were naked, they wither; they just don't last.

My sister, whether you have been hurt in business, in a relationship, in church or your family God is an amazing healer. He has the ability to reach down and touch you right where you are hurting by His Holy Spirit. Today, reach out to Father God and ask Him to soften your heart, and as you do ask Him to protect it and be the keeper of it. I trust God to keep anything on my behalf. Similarly, for those of you reading that don't immediately think you have hardened your heart, ask God to show you any areas where your heart has become calloused. Let me give you an example.

Some years ago I went to a healing retreat where you are assigned counsellors to pray with you and seek God with you for deliverance in your life. At the time I went I knew I had a call to ministry and wanted to make sure I was healed before I started working with others (I've since learned it's an ongoing process). It was a weekend event and during the first day we talked a lot. They prayed with me and none of us were receiving anything at that time that needed to be dealt with. By the afternoon of the second day I started to feel really good thinking, 'Wow, I'm all good and really ready for ministry' – or so I thought. They asked me again in the afternoon if God had revealed anything to me and I said He hadn't so we began to just have a general talk. All of a sudden one of the counsellors said to me, 'Will you forgive my race for all they have done to your race, for every act of racism, bias and hurt?' I went to say yes because I didn't have a problem with that, and as I was opening my mouth to say yes, I began to weep. All of a sudden I started to remember incidents in school, in work and socially where I had felt excluded or discriminated against because of my colour. God moved in and brought healing. Afterwards, I just could not believe it, when I say I wept, I wept!!! This was hidden deep within me and I wasn't conscious of it. Somewhere along the line I had protected myself, but that day the Lord was saying, now is the time for your deliverance. If you had asked me prior to that weekend if there was any area that I thought might come up, that wouldn't have even entered my list. Every so often God shows me something else He wants to heal in my life and I've learnt to just allow Him to be God because you feel that much lighter when He's finished with you.

Lastly, Rahab demonstrated that she was stronger than she thought. She said their hearts melted until no courage remained, yet she turned away the king's men, hid two spies, negotiated an escape route and plan for her and her entire family – she was stronger than she thought!

Woman of destiny, you are stronger than you think. Though the seas have roared, the fires of raged against you, you have stood, and no matter what condition you might think you are in, you are still here and standing! You are still here and pressing on. Where many would have given up, daughter of destiny, you are still pushing ahead, still getting up another day hopeful that your change is going come!

Real woman of destiny, truly your change is going to come, where you are is not where you're going to be – be encouraged!

Real women of destiny are not hard-hearted!

1. Has your heart become hard?

2. Are there any issues that you need to seek the Lord's healing for?

3. What, if any, are your self-protection mechanisms?

4. God wants to bring healing to your life, will you let Him?

Lesson 15 Real women of destiny communicate

'And as soon as we heard these things, our hearts melted; neither did there remain any more courage in anyone because of you, for the Lord your God, He is God in heaven above and on earth beneath.
Joshua 2: 11

A real woman of destiny is an effective communicator. Rahab was an effective communicator, she listened without interrupting the king's men or the spies, she gave clear directions and instructions, she negotiated her terms and she made her requests. Real women of destiny need to be able to communicate effectively if they are to arrive at their pre ordained destination in Christ.

Something else Rahab did was articulate her feelings, she didn't leave it to the spies to mind read what she wanted in return for her kindness. Rahab said, Our hearts melted, and there was no more courage left in us.'. She didn't do the silent treatment that some of us like to do, expecting others to automatically know how to meet our needs. She spoke up, she said what was wrong. Real woman of destiny, when you have a problem with something or someone, speak up, articulate it – how else will they know what you're thinking? Women who don't know their power and don't know who they are, are frightened of repercussions and rejection so they keep their thoughts and feelings hidden, and some even plot revenge.

Sister, learn to articulate your feelings! I know many a man, and fellow sister for that matter, who have gone through the day, week and even life wondering what they did to upset someone. If you are a real woman of destiny that 'someone' shouldn't be you; you should be able to communicate your feelings!

A part of effective communication is the ability to give constructive feedback. This can be challenging, especially if it is to someone you care about. The reality is that if you care about them you will give them feedback. Let me share another management development tool with you, it is a **Five Step Model** that will help you to give constructive feedback when necessary. This will help stop you from carrying unnecessary baggage.

1. **CHOOSE THE RIGHT TIME AND PLACE...** When you have made the decision to give someone feedback, make sure it is not in front of others where appropriate. No one likes to be embarrassed in front of others, so choose a time and a place that is appropriate. I say where appropriate because there are times when I give feedback publicly because there is learning for all that are in attendance. However, if it is personal it is important to make a point of finding an appropriate place to do it. This is both for praise and areas a person may need to develop in. The right time is important as we learnt in Lesson 11. Ensure when you are giving someone feedback that you are not stressed or emotional as this can detract from the point you are trying to raise.

2   **START IN A POSITIVE WAY...** No one likes to feel attacked or only hear what they are doing wrong so it's important to let people know what they are doing right as well. Indicate their good points and a possible good outcome. This will stop the recipient of your feedback from getting defensive. How many times has someone come to you and said, 'Why didn't you do this or that?' Our immediate response is often to defend ourselves and retaliate by saying, 'Well you don't do it either or look who's talking?' Start positively and people are much more likely to listen and respond constructively to your comments.

3   **BE SPECIFIC...** When you are giving feedback be specific, give dates, times, figures, and frequency if possible. This will stop any disputes about what you are saying and put the details right into the mind of the recipient. For example, 'Susie, on Wednesday the 8 June, when I came to your office, you gave me a cup of water to drink. I was so thankful and it's not the only time you have looked after me or been hospitable. I want to take this opportunity to say thank you for your service, it is so appreciated.'

Feedback doesn't always have to be a negative! After this interaction, Susie knows exactly what she did, when she did it, and how I felt about it.

4, **TAKE RESPONSIBILITY...**It's important that when we are giving someone constructive feedback that we acknowledge our part in the situation; where possible don't involve others, just keep it to you and that person. When we involve others by saying things like, 'Well I'm not the only one that thinks this, everyone else does as well!' we can damage their confidence and esteem. All of sudden they start to feel that everyone has been talking about them and they automatically become defensive. Even if everyone else agrees with what you are saying, you don't have to be their spokesperson. Let them speak for themselves. Take responsibility and remember to allow the other person to say what they think. You may find that you have contributed to a situation more than you had originally thought!

5   **FOCUS ON BEHAVIOUR...**When we focus on behaviour and not personality our interaction is less likely to turn into an argument because what we think of someone's personality is subjective, not objective. An example of focusing on behaviour is, 'Susie, I really appreciate you giving me a lift to church, however, when you arrive late to pick me up, it makes me feel anxious because I like to be on time. In future can we arrange to meet earlier so we arrive at church in good time?' This is a good example of constructive feedback. Here's the scenario in a destructive or negative way, 'Susie, why are you always late? We always get to church late. Can't you come round earlier?' I know which one I would receive better, how about you?

Real women of destiny communicate!

1. How well do you communicate with others?

2. What do you need to improve on?

3. How well do you communicate your feelings?

4. Is there anyone you need to give some constructive feedback to, whether positive or developmental?

5. Is there anyone you need to forgive? Sometimes we think it's the other person when really we are the one who is not communicating!

Lesson 16   A real woman of destiny is Kingdom-minded

'Now therefore, I beg you, swear to me by the Lord, since I have shown you kindness, that you also will show kindness to my father's house, and give me a true token.

'and spare my father, my mother, my brothers, my sisters and all that they have, and deliver our lives from death.'
Joshua 2: 12- 13 NKJV

Rahab negotiated being saved from death. She could quite easily have made sure she was okay and escaped but she didn't, she was thinking about her whole family. I believe Rahab had been waiting for this moment her whole life. Who knows whether she was the main breadwinner for her family, but whatever the case she was concerned about them and all they had. This is someone who is a kingdom-thinker. A kingdom-thinker doesn't just concern themselves with their own lives, ministries, issues, hopes, and pains but they're concerned about the whole body of Christ. They are concerned about nations dying, they're concerned about seeing His kingdom come on earth as it is heaven. They preserve and prepare for the next generation; they don't just eat all they have with no thought for tomorrow. They plan and prepare through teaching and ministry; they write books and diaries so that truths can be passed on; they disciple and mentor so what they have learnt is not lost.

Rahab couldn't leave her family because she was a kingdom-thinker. I can imagine the conversations she had with her mother and father, where they have asked her, 'Daughter, when are you going to give up this life, it's no good, it's dangerous out there, you don't know who will knock your door. Your sisters are growing up we don't want them to see you in this role. Daughter, you could be killed, look at Susie, she's a dressmaker, she makes good money, her parents are so proud of her. Rahab, Rahab are you listening to us?'

Only Rahab has long since stopped listening. She knows her parents mean well, she knows they worry but destiny is in her belly. She thinks, 'If only they could understand that I'm not doing this just for me but for them as well. I know this is where I am now but this is not where I'm going to be, destiny is calling me, I just want to be in the right place to listen.' And one day she hears the story of how the God of Israel dried up the waters in the Red sea and she realises that this is it, that's how she'll get out, it will be with the help of the God of Israel. She just has to find a way of finding favour with Him.

'Yes mother, yes father, I hear you, it won't be long, I wont' be doing this much longer, we'll get out of here soon.'

Her mother and father probably looked at each other with a knowing look because they have heard this dream of hers so many times before, yet she remains a harlot in the city. Nevertheless, they love her and go about their way hoping for her and praying for her in their own way.

When a real woman of destiny is a Kingdom-thinker she has to live with misunderstanding. If we look through the bible it is littered with people who were misunderstood yet they had a destiny, people like Moses, Paul, David, the list goes on and on. So my sister, if you have felt like no one understands you, no one quite gets what you are sensing in your belly, they may have looked at your current circumstance and called you a dreamer, don't let that discourage you, continue to think Kingdom, continue to think beyond where you are, for a real woman of destiny is not 'me, me, me'!!! She's a family-thinker, a community-thinker, a Kingdom-thinker a body-thinker!!!

Let me ask you something woman of destiny. What have you been dreaming of? What break or opportunity have you been waiting to happen to save you and your family?

Don't let it die if God has put it in you, it will surely come to pass. The bible says in Luke 1: 45,

'Blessed is she who believed, for there will be a fulfilment of those things which were told her from the Lord.'

Real women of destiny are Kingdom-minded!

1. Have you been Kingdom-minded?

2. What can you start or develop to prepare for the next generation?

3. Who can help you?

4. How can you involve your whole family?

5. What is your circle of influence and how will you tap into it?

Lesson 17   A real woman of destiny doesn't gossip

So the men answered her, 'Our lives for yours, if none of you tell this business of ours. And it shall be, when the Lord has given us the land, that we will deal kindly and truly with you.'
Joshua 2:14 NKJV

After Rahab had negotiated a safe passage for her and her family the spies gave her the conditions on which they would keep their word. They said if she or her family don't tell anyone else about their business it will be done, God will deal kindly with her. In other words, don't gossip!

Gossiping is the act of spreading news from person to person, especially rumors or private information. (Other words are hearsay, tittle-tattle, scandal and chit chat.)

A real woman knows how to keep confidences. She's not a gossip. So many of us would have wanted to tell everyone how we fed and looked after the men of God and how they are coming back for us – but not Rahab. Not a real woman of destiny! Even if we weren't so obvious we would start to ask questions of our girlfriends, like 'So what are they saying around town about the king's men coming to my inn', 'Did they mention me?', 'Did they say that the spies were from Israel where they serve the God that dries up seas?' When our girlfriends ask why we're asking, we'd have that little 'I know something you don't know' smile' or tone and then say, 'Oh nothing, I was just wondering!' The bible says:

Death and life are in the power of the tongue.
Proverbs 18:21

A tale barer reveals secrets, but he who is of a faithful spirit conceals a matter.
Proverbs 11:13

Rahab wasn't a talebearer, neither are real women of destiny. I know how difficult it is sometimes when you know or have a piece of information that you are bursting to share with someone else. We have to check what the cause is for doing this – one reason may be acceptance. Subconsciously or in some cases consciously we are saying, 'Do they know who I am? Do they like me? Do they respect me? Do they think I know what I'm talking about? Do they think I'm attractive? Do they want to be with me?' The lower our self-esteem is, the more we worry about things like that, but all of us give some thought to them. We want to make ourselves look better and gain greater acceptance. There are some people who thrive on having pieces of information that they dish out if you're good enough, if you're in their clique, and all the time you are feeling excluded. Don't take it personally – it's not about you but about the person gossiping; it's about their need to be important and popular.

Another possibility is that we have not developed our minds to the extent that we have anything else to talk about but people. Somebody once suggested that people with great minds talk about ideas, people with average minds talk about events, and people with small minds talk about other people. Real women of destiny need to strive to have great minds!

If you are reading this and recognise that you are guilty of gossiping, I believe there is a cure, here are some useful steps:

1. Repent – ask God to forgive you for being a talebearer and for using your tongue to carry tittle-tattle and rumours.

2. Ask the Lord to help you guard your tongue. The psalmist did. 'Let the words of my mouth and the meditation of my heart be acceptable in Thy sight, O LORD, my rock and my Redeemer.' (Psalm 19:14). 'Set a guard, O LORD, over my mouth; Keep watch over the door of my lips.' (Psalm 141:3). God loves to help people who humbly admit their need and ask Him for help. Will you try it? He will help you conquer the gossip habit.

3. Develop our self-esteem – when we feel good about ourselves, fear of exclusion, putting others down, gossiping and so forth, is far less appealing.

4. If you know a piece of information to be true go to the person in private and confront them – 'And if your brother sins, go and reprove him in private; if he listens to you, you have won your brother.' (Matthew 18:15).

5. Refuse to listen to it. 'He who goes about as a slanderer reveals secrets, therefore do not associate with one who flatters with their lips.' **(Proverbs 20:19)**. If all of us would follow that advice, the gossipers would have nobody to gossip to. Tell the person to go and talk to who they're talking about or simply change the subject by saying I don't feel comfortable talking about this. This is particularly hard when it's juicy but the more you do it the easier it gets and the less people come to you with it!

6. Be more open and transparent. Instead of us acting like we've got it all together, we suggest that we're not perfect either.

7. Learn to love. We learn that primarily by observing God's love for us (cf. 1 John 4:19). And when we truly learn it, we will not gossip any more. 'Hatred stirs up strife, but love covers all transgressions.' (Proverbs 10:12) That idea was borrowed by Peter who said, 'Above all, keep fervent in your love for one another, because love covers a multitude of sins.' (1 Peter 4:8) The worst thing about gossip is that it is totally unloving. We are showing no loving consideration whatsoever for the person we talk about in a derogatory manner. We are tearing him down before others, whereas love builds him up (cf. 1 Corinthians 8:1).

Before we open our mouths it might be good to ask, 'Will this build respect for the person I am about to mention? Will it build trust? Will it build love?' If not, it would be better to leave it unsaid.

A real woman of destiny doesn't gossip

Selah! Pause and think on this!

Lesson 18 A real woman of destiny takes action

Then she let them down by a rope through the window, for her house was on the city wall; she dwelt on the wall.
Joshua 2: 15 NKJV

The bible says that Rahab let the spies down by rope. This means she didn't go and get someone else to supervise the lowering of the men, she personally let them down by rope! It's amazing how when destiny is calling we find the strength to take action. I don't know if or how Rahab had been looking after herself because the bible doesn't say how big or fit she or the spies were, but she would have had to balance the weight of two men tied around something sturdy to let them down. You need strength to take action! I wonder how much practice she had gained doing this over her years as a prostitute. How many times a wife had come knocking at the door looking for her husband who she believed was frequenting Rahab's premises. I wonder if this was the first time she had ever done this or whether she had been prepared over the years.

Whatever the case, Rahab took action, she didn't wait for thunder and lightening to occur, she didn't wait for a strapping young man to come in and help her lower them down. She dug deep and heaved them down out of the window and onto the wall. Sister, you know there are some things that you are waiting for the Lord to do in your life and He is saying, 'I'm waiting for you to take action'.

It's funny, I remember having a dream that was similar to one of those 'Romancing the stone' films (it's a bit like a treasure hunt movie for those of you who don't know), and I've since heard others share similar experiences and visions from the Lord. As a young Christian this was my experience. I dreamt that I was on a ship and I was being asked to walk the plank, a long piece of wood that went out into the sea, and I was saying to myself, 'No way, there's nothing to walk on.' I heard a voice behind me saying, 'Will you step out?' I eventually realised that it was the Lord and I said, 'I can't, there's no plank.' The Lord then said to me again, 'Will you step out?' Again, I was thinking no way, I'll drown! Then the Lord said, 'Do you trust me?' I thought about it and said, 'Yes.' 'Then walk the plank,' he responded. I cautiously put one foot out and there the plank appeared. I put the next foot out and then more of the plank appeared. When I stopped, the plank stopped extending. I then woke up. It was God's way of telling me that if I wanted to serve Him and do all the things I believe He has called me to do and be, I have to step out, I have to do something. Can you imagine what would have happened if I hadn't trusted God and stepped out?

Number one my sister, you probably would not be reading this book or any others in the Deep Calleth Unto Deep series. Number two, you probably would never have received some of the revelations and deliverance I believe God has used this ministry bring forth.

Real woman of destiny, it's time to step out. Let me share something with you about the writing of this book. I had gone away to a Christian retreat for three days to seek God as to my next move. I had so many things on my plate that I couldn't think which one to do first. I laid everything out before the Lord and asked which one I should begin to work on first. He said none of them. I was curious, because I was thinking, 'I'm at breaking point right now and I shouldn't do anything?' I thought, 'Oh great, maybe I can rest then.' But no, the Lord began to stir the words of this book and instead of taking away things and giving me direction on what I was already doing, He gave me more!!!! Only my Daddy in heaven could do that. One thing I know is, as I've taken action to write this book, I'm amazed at what I can do in a short space of time with divine unction and prayers! Some of you may be waiting for direction on what to do with what's already on your plate and He's saying, 'I'll attend to those things but first you must do this or that…'

Woman of God, it's time for action! I know some people struggle at times like me with when to wait and when to take action. Joyce Meyer, an awesome woman of God, helped me with this. She said, 'If we're going the wrong way, God is big enough to find us!' Sister, if you step out and it's not where or what God had for you, He's big enough to find you!

REAL WOMEN of destiny, know when to DO and when to just BE!

So are you ready? If so, go to **Appendix 3** where I have provided you with a template of an action plan. Seek the Lord about what He would have you do and develop a plan of action. Don't wait, but plan your next steps or else procrastination will creep in and leave you doing and being everything other than what God has called you to. Women of action don't procrastinate and if they do it's not for long. Have a look at the following types of procrastination traps and identify which one hinders you. When you find out pray about it and make a change by taking action. Let that be your first objective in your plan – stop procrastinating!

- **SELF DOUBTER**

Despite professional or personal competence and ability to do good work this person often doubts their capability. Work and opportunities are avoided in case the results further damage their self-esteem. A good example of this is a task that involves public exposure: public speaking or writing for publication. The fear of publicly failing takes over so the task is avoided.

- **PERFECTIONIST**

The search for perfection is a mechanism to avoid failure. Perfectionists set high standards for themselves and often for other people. The outcome is that they will always need more information, better trained workers, more time, more creative ideas… more, more more. In short, there will always be something more needed before a goal can be achieved, so it never is.

- **REBEL**

This one expresses defiance of others. They try to demonstrate self-control and determination over people and environments. The rebel likes crises and problems that can be solved in order to show control over events. It's also legitimate procrastination! A good example of rebel behaviour is the last minute deadline or the large task attempted in short time periods.

EXCESSIVE SOCIALISER

Here the procrastinator delays the start or finish of any activity by involving themselves in conversation (or gossip – if this is the case or you go back and read Lesson 17). Lengthy non-work related chat, or trips around the office or trivial tasks... anything to avoid getting started.

DAYDREAMER

There is always a distraction to break concentration, and wander off into a daydream about – future career, family, friends, social events and so on... Whatever the work, distractions are always there. It suggests a lack of concentration or discipline or commitment to focusing on the task or work.

PRIORITY INVERTER

This is a very typical form of procrastination for managers or people who have a wide range of tasks to perform. It is easier to sit down and do the minor tasks – which don't take long before tackling the more important ones. Except they always take longer than they expected. And so more important tasks are often rushed or aren't completed on time...

All the various forms of procrastination, whether it be natural and creative or more deeply rooted in our work or life style (the doubter, perfectionist, rebel, and excessive socialiser), can be made to sound plausible. But, more often than not, they are excuses to avoid failure in the eyes of ourselves and others.

A real woman of destiny takes action!

1. What have you been putting off that you know the Lord has called you to do?

2. What will stop you from stepping out?

3. Are the things that will stop you stepping out excuses o genuine obstacles?

4. Are you serious about being a real woman of destiny?

5. If the answer is yes, then it's time to take out your Action Plan (**Appendix 3**) and start planning your way forward with the Lord!

Lesson 19   A real woman of destiny has faith

Then she said, 'According to your words, so be it.' And she sent them away and they departed. And she bound the scarlet cord in the window.
Joshua 2: 21 NKJV

This lesson is very simple. Much has been written in the Christian world about faith but it is crucial that I include it within this book because real women of destiny have faith. They take God at His word, what He said He would do they believe He will do! Hebrews 11: 6 says, *'But without faith it is impossible to please Him, for He who comes to God must believe that He is, and that He is a rewarder of those who diligently seek Him.'* Rahab believed that He was and is, she exercised faith and as a result pleased God. You see, after Rahab had negotiated her and her family's safety, to confirm what they said would happen she simply said, 'According to your words so be it.' Do you know how many people would have wanted a signed oath, or asked them to leave their stick or something of value to ensure they came back for them? Not Rahab, not a real woman of destiny, they have faith, they let their yes be yes and their no, no! All of this from a local harlot!

Rahab's faith didn't allow her to question how, when or why. She just trusted that the God of the spies would be honourable. Isn't that interesting? I know Christians who have been saved all their lives who don't exercise that kind of faith. They still question, double guess, are uncertain the minute the going gets tough, yet this woman, who had only heard second hand what this God of Israel could do, was willing to put her life on it! Lord, have mercy on us!

Father even now I ask for you to have mercy on us, where we have had little faith, where we have doubted, where we have believed everybody else's report except yours. We ask you to forgive us. Lord we repent in the name of Jesus, we are sorry. Father. Where we have moaned, complained, been distrustful and ungrateful when you did not move in the way we had wanted you to and then we so quickly lost faith. Father will you forgive us, we ask you now by your Holy Spirit to stir us afresh, stir up our faith account in You, in Jesus name. Father, some of us only have a mustard seed of faith available and even with that Lord Your word says that we can move mountains. Stir us afresh Lord, in Jesus name we pray! Amen.

Without faith it is impossible to please Him!

Real women of destiny have faith!

1. Do you have faith?

2. What stops you from having faith?

3. What can you do to increase your faith? For example, reading scriptures and books by those who have stepped out by faith, by learning to trust God one step at a time.

4. Who can help you increase your faith?

Lesson 20   Real women of destiny reach their destination

Now the city shall be doomed by the Lord to destruction, it and all who are in it. Only Rahab the harlot shall live, she and all who are with her in the house, because she hid the messengers of God.
Joshua Chapter 6: 17

Real women of destiny reach their destiny. They arrive at the place where they should be, not forever wondering, pondering and asking where they should be. They seek God concerning their destinies and arrive at it with confidence and assurance, not second guessing, constantly checking they are in the right place out of fear, but out of humility and desire to be where the Father is.

Rahab arrived at her destination because she was obedient to everything the spies had told her. She had put the scarlet cord in the window, she had gathered her family and everyone that was to be saved in one place and was ready when the spies came. How many times have you experienced going on a coach trip or journey with a number of people. We are all asked to be at the meeting point for a set time, let's say 7.00am and when 7.00am comes we're busy waiting for sister so and so, they're late, again! Woman of destiny, if one person had been late for that trip that Rahab was about to embark on, they would have been utterly destroyed – think about that the next time you are asked to arrive somewhere at a given time!

Rahab arrived at her destiny by being obedient, not partially but fully – that's if there's such a thing as partial obedience because you are either obeying the Lord's command fully or not.

Rahab arrived at her destination because she kept her word, she didn't gossip, she prepared her family, she did everything that was asked of her. No double crossing, no adding on to the negotiations but she kept her word. To arrive at your destination you must have integrity – do what you say you're going to do, how you said you'd do it, when you said you'd do it and where you said you'd do it.

Real women of destiny arrive at their destination with integrity.

Rahab arrived at her destination because she trusted the spies and their God, that what they said they would do, they would do.

Real women of destiny trust others. They're not foolish with who they trust and for what but when it matters they don't let issues of the past hinder their ability to trust.

Real women of destiny trust God above all else.

Rahab was a prostitute yet she dealt with the king's men and the two spies with dignity. She didn't allow what she did to affect where she was going. She didn't allow where she was coming from to affect her self-esteem, self worth, self-image or expectancy of where she was going. So many women allow what they do or where they are coming from affect how they feel about themselves and so forever feel unworthy. Unworthy to be used by God, unworthy to experience the blessings He desires to pour out on them. Real women of destiny don't let what they do or how they feel about themselves to cloud the bigger picture of where they are going. Rahab had an appointment with destiny – she was preparing to enter the lineage of the King of Kings!

Real women of destiny don't allow the past to affect their self esteem, worth or image.

I don't believe Rahab knew exactly where she was going when she left Jericho. She just went out with her family wherever she was sent by the spies. She didn't need the address, the where or the how, she just needed to know that she was sent and the God of Israel had saved her.

Real women of destiny are sent and they are saved.

Real women of destiny reach their destination!

1. Do you know your destination?

2. How will you know you have arrived if you don't know where you're going?

3. Complete the Personal Development Plan in **Appendix 4** as a guide to helping you identify, where you're coming from, where you're going, how you're going to get there, and how you'll know you've arrived!

Part **3** Will the REAL WOMEN
of Destiny Please
Stand UP?

The Impact of not being real on others

My sister, as we draw close to the end of this Volume there are a few more things we need to be aware of when we are getting ready to stand up as real women of destiny. My sister, when you are not a real woman of destiny it impacts those around you, your family, friends, church, colleagues and partners. Some of the ways it impacts them is as follows:

1. When you are not honest with your feelings it can be frustrating to those around you. They know that you are feeling something or that you are dissatisfied and if those around you don't know who they are and whose they are, they can begin to think that they have done something to upset or offend you. When they are in the dark for too long it can end in separation, physically and/or emotionally because they never feel as though you approve of them.

2. When you are not a real woman of destiny you can end up being dishonest. I don't believe this is done consciously but because you don't know who you are, you end up adopting other people's personalities; you can almost pick and choose who you become. The challenge with this is that you are not being who God created you to be – you are a counterfeit of you. I don't know if you have ever been given counterfeit money, you feel so aggrieved, even if it's only fifty pence, you feel so cheated. You start wondering who gave it to you as you track back all the stores you have been in and anyone you have exchanged money with. How much more living with a counterfeit! Everything's the same but something's missing. I remember seeing an advert for a movie where I think it was aliens that had taken over a family or town (don't quote me) but in the advert for the film, one of the aliens that had taken over a family went to kiss the daughter in the house and the little girl turned round to her said 'Mummy, you smell different.' The person was able to counterfeit everything but there will always be a flaw. In this case it was a smell. My sister, people can always smell a forgery, it's just a matter of

time. They carry on, they think, there's something that doesn't quite sit with that person and eventually they realise, they're not real!

3. Another impact on those around you when you're not a real woman of destiny is that you may set unrealistic expectations of them. When you are not sure where you fit or where you belong, you can put pressure on others to be like what you either hoped you'd be like or what you think everyone else thinks they should be like. Never allowing your loved ones to just be. Sisters, there is an impact on those around you when you're not a real woman of destiny!

4. When you are not being a real woman of destiny your loved ones can feel cheated. They see your potential, they see your abilities, your talents and gifts and so they feel cheated when you settle for less. Sister, be careful because when you stay where you are, not fulfilling your potential and purpose you are cheating not only your loved ones, but every person you were supposed to impact with your presence and your ministry.

5. We can become controlling when we are not real women of destiny. You see, we control our image, what we put out, how we are perceived, you name it – a spirit of control can attach itself with the promise of keeping you safe from being exposed. My sister, always side with God, there are more for you than there are against you. Control and manipulation are not your portion but freedom and destiny are yours in Jesus name.

6. Where we are not walking as real women of destiny we can harbour feelings of anger and bitterness. The bible says we ought to, 'Look carefully lest anyone fall short of the grace of God; lest any root of bitterness spring up causing trouble and by this many become defiled.' (Hebrews 12:15) Sisters, we must look carefully lest the sight of someone else's progression cause bitterness to spring up. You can feel as though you haven't done something or you owe them something

7.   Finally, when we are not being real women of God people never truly get to know us because we don't know ourselves. We are so busy trying to mask our vulnerabilities and issues that they only ever get to know who we have presented to them. My sister, the bible says, 'You are fearfully and wonderfully made!' (Psalm 139:14)

Who God created you to be is perfect, everything about you is by design, the shape of your nose, bottom and ears, all of it was created by design. The sound of your voice, the style of your hair, all of it He says is fearfully and wonderfully made. It's time to stop hiding my sister, come out for the world is waiting for you and your gift!

My sister destiny awaits you, and so do your loved ones, arise!

Will the REAL WOMEN of Destiny Please Stand Up?

> *By faith the harlot Rahab did not perish with those who did not believe, when she received the spies with peace.*
> **Hebrews 11:31**

The bible says that Rahab did not perish with those who didn't believe but she received the spies with peace, how beautiful. She didn't perish and neither will you. Rahab made a stand for her family, her destiny and her children's children, will you?

Rahab received the spies with peace. I love that, she received them with peace, peace means, *calm, freedom from strife, reconciliation and an absence of war*. My sister, for some of you there has been a war raging within you for your destiny. Every time you get ready to step out into your destiny war rages, war in your mind, war in your household, war on your job, war in your church. I understand and so does God, however, He says, 'Today receive your destiny, direction and hope again with peace, not the kind of peace the world gives but the peace that Jesus gives to you.' My sister, will you receive your destiny and hope again with peace?

Rahab did not perish with those who did not believe. She wasn't found with those who were saying, 'What if He doesn't show up?' 'What if you fail?' 'What if you don't make it?' No, she wasn't caught with the doubters, sister, and today the Lord would say to you, 'Daughter, whose report will you believe? Will you dare to dream again, will you dare to believe again?'

Rahab received the spies, receive means to *take delivery of, obtain and accept*. Sister, Daddy God has a delivery for you. Are you willing to receive it, are you willing to accept it? Not only does He have eternal life for you but He has hope for you, you just have to receive it. Sometimes when we have been in a place for too long, we forget how to receive, we forget how to get good gifts without wondering what the catch is, or what the cost is. My sister, His gifts are without repentance – He gives and never takes them back. Will you accept His gifts? His gifts of the Spirit? Will you accept His gift of unconditional love? Sister will you receive again?

There are some of you reading this book that have dreamt of being in politics, in school governances to make a difference, some of you have dreamt of being in the community and legal system.

Sisters, it's time to stand up! It's time to take action and go where the Lord has called you to.

Sisters from the north, the south, the east and the west,

> *Arise, shine; For your light has come!*
> *And the glory of the Lord is risen upon you.*
> **Isaiah 60:1**

Real women of destiny,

> *The Gentiles shall see your righteousness,*
> *And all kings your glory,*
> *You shall be called by a new name.*
> *You shall also be a crown of glory in the hand of the Lord,*
> *A royal diadem in the hand of your God.*
> *You shall no longer be termed forsaken,*
> *Nor shall your land anymore be termed desolate,*
> *But you shall be called Hephzibah (my delight is in her),*
> *and your land Beulah;*
> *For the Lord delights in you,*
> *And your land shall be married.*
> *For as a young man marries a virgin,*
> *So shall your sons marry you;*
> *And as the bridegroom rejoices over the bride,*
> *So shall your God rejoice over you.*
> **Isaiah 62: 2-6**

Sisters, 'stand' means to *rise, get up, stand up, arise and get to your feet.*

Sisters, we're getting ready to stand up together as REAL WOMAN of destiny!

Now if you are ready to go to the next level, if you are ready to take on board the lessons learnt within this book, if you're ready to wave this book as a flag and make a prophetic declaration that you are not staying where you are, and if it costs you, it costs you, then it leaves me with one final question:

Will the REAL WOMEN of destiny now please stand up?

Sisters from Ghana – Megyina pintiin

Sisters from Spanish speaking countries

- Yo me paro
- Estoy estando parado para arriba

Sisters from Brazil (Portuguese) – Eu estou estando acima

Sisters from Europe:

- The UK – I'm standing up!
- France – Je me leve
- Portugal – Levanto-me
- Germany – Ich steche auf
- Dutch – Ik laat zitten

Sisters from Nigeria – Mo duro fun Jesu
Mo dide fun Jesu

Sisters from America – I'm standing up!

Sisters from the North, South, East and West:
WE'RE STANDING UP as REAL WOMEN of Destiny!!!

Hallelujah!!! Glory to God!

Prayer of commitment

When all has been said, when all the lessons have been learnt there is only really one life changing thing you can do next and that is pray, and as you pray this prayer with me believe what you are saying, invite the Holy Spirit to join you, and feel His comfort around you.

Dear Lord and Father in heaven,

Thank you for life,
Thank you for destiny and hope,
Thank you that you are a life changing God.
Lord, I admit that I have sinned and gone my own way,
I have sold my talents, gifts and value for less than your intended worth for me, I am sorry!
I confess the times that I knowingly and unknowingly hid my true self to be accepted by man,
I need your forgiveness.
I am willing to turn away from all that I know is wrong, that includes the things that I have convinced myself is right, because I want to go with you
I want you to be first in my life.
Thank you for dying on the cross to take away my sins.
Thank you for your gift of forgiveness, wholeness and a new life.
I now take your gift.
I ask you to come into my life by your Holy Spirit.
Come in to fill my life.
Come in as my Saviour, Counsellor and Lord forever.
I thank you Lord Jesus.
Amen

If you have taken this step of faith for the first time, find yourself a church where you can meet other Christians and find out more about Jesus Christ.

Then purchase a bible so that you can discover what God wants to say to you.

Learning Styles – General Descriptions

Activists

Activists involve themselves fully and without bias in new experiences. They enjoy the here and now and are happy to be dominated by immediate experiences. They are open-minded, not sceptical, and this tends to make them enthusiastic about anything new. Their philosophy is 'I'll try anything once'. They tend to act first and consider consequences afterwards. Their days are filled with activity. They tackle problems by brainstorming. As soon as the excitement from one activity has died down they are busy looking for the next. They tend to thrive on the challenge of new experiences but are bored with implementation and longer term consolidation. They are gregarious people constantly involving themselves with others but, in doing so, they seek to centre all activities around themselves.

Reflectors

Reflectors like to stand back to ponder experiences and observe them from many different perspectives. They collect data, both first hand and from others, and prefer to think about it thoroughly before coming to any conclusion. The thorough collection and analysis of data about experiences and events is what counts so they tend to postpone reaching definitive conclusions for as long as possible. Their philosophy is to be cautious. They are thoughtful people who like to consider all possible angles and implications before making a move. They prefer to take a back seat in meetings and discussions. They enjoy observing other people in action. They listen to others and get the drift of the discussion before making their own points. They tend to adopt a low profile and have a slightly distant, tolerant, unruffled air about them. When they act it is as part of a wide picture which includes the past as well as the present and others' observations as well as their own.

Theorists

Theorists adapt and integrate observations into complex but logically sound theories. They think problems through in a vertical step by step logical way. They assimilate disparate facts into coherent theories. They tend to be perfectionists who won't rest easy until things are tidy and fit into their rational scheme. They like to analyse and synthesise. They are keen on basic assumptions, principles, theories models and systems thinking. Their philosophy prizes rationality and logic 'If it's logical it's good'. Questions they frequently ask are: 'Does it make sense?', 'How does this fit with that?', 'What are the basic assumptions?' They tend to be detached, analytical and dedicated to rational objectivity rather than anything subjective or ambiguous. Their approach to problems is consistently logical. This is their 'mental set' and they rigidly reject anything that doesn't fit with it. They prefer to maximise certainty and feel uncomfortable with subjective judgements, lateral thinking and anything flippant.

Pragmatists

Pragmatists are keen on trying out ideas, theories and techniques to see if they work in practice. They positively search out new ideas and take the first opportunity to experiment with applications. They are the sort of people who return from management courses brimming with new ideas that they want to try out in practice. They like to get on with things and act quickly and confidently on ideas that attract them. They tend to be impatient with ruminating and open-ended discussions. They are essentially practical, down to earth people who like making practical decisions and solving problems. They respond to problems and opportunities 'as a challenge'. Their philosophy is: 'There is always a better way' and 'If it works it's good'.

© Honey and Mumford 1986

If you would like to find out more about your personal learning style, there is a questionnaire that you can purchase and complete, go to <u>www.peterhoney.com</u>

Building a Johari window

You can use the Johari Window model to examine the level of openness and self-disclosure in your own relationships.

1. Draw three Johari Windows, representing the relationship between you and church, work and family/friends.

Church

2. Describe which parts of yourself you keep in the hidden area. Explain your reasons for doing so. Describe the costs or benefits or both of not disclosing these parts of yourself.

3. Look at the blind area of your model. Is this area large or small because of the amount of feedback (much or little) that you get from your partner or because of your willingness to receive the feedback that is offered?

4.   Explain whether or not you are satisfied with the results illustrated by your answers. If you are not satisfied, explain what you can do to remedy the problem.

Work

```



```

5.   Describe which parts of yourself you keep in the hidden area. Explain your reasons for doing so. Describe the costs or benefits or both of not disclosing these parts of yourself.

6.   Look at the blind area of your model. Is this area large or small because of the amount of feedback (much or little) that you get from your partner or because of your willingness to receive the feedback that is offered?

7.   Explain whether or not you are satisfied with the results illustrated by your answers. If you are not satisfied, explain what you can do to remedy the problem.

Family/Friends

8. Describe which parts of yourself you keep in the hidden area. Explain your reasons for doing so. Describe the costs or benefits or both of not disclosing these parts of yourself.

9. Look at the blind area of your model. Is this area large or small because of the amount of feedback (much or little) that you get from your partner or because of your willingness to receive the feedback that is offered?

10. Explain whether or not you are satisfied with the results illustrated by your answers. If you are not satisfied, explain what you can do to remedy the problem.

REAL WOMAN of Destiny Action Plan

Name: Date: Review:

Action/Objective	Achieve by (Date)	Who will help? (Name)	Reward for completing

REAL WOMAN of Destiny Action Plan

Name: Date: Review:

Action/Objective	Achieve by (Date)	Who will help? (Name)	Reward for completing

Personal Development Plan

1. **Reviewing where you are and where you want to get to?**
    (Where have you been? Life experiences, jobs, skills you have etc. What's going well in your work and life in general? What's made you who you are – positive and negative?)

2. **What could be improved?**
    (What do you have control over, e.g. Attitude, behaviour, response to situations and organisation?)

3. **Where do you want to get to?**
   (Where do you see yourself in five years time? Identifying individual hopes and aspirations for home, work, ministry etc.)

4. **How will you get there?**
   (What resources do you need to achieve your goals, what mentors, experience, attitudes, behaviours, skills, qualifications etc?)

5. **How will you know you have arrived?**
   (How will you know you have achieved your goals? What feelings, skills, attitude, behaviour and feedback from others will you receive?)

About the author

Jacqueline Peart

Inspirational ◆ Speaker ◆ Poet ◆ Author ◆ Trainer

Jacqueline is the youngest of three sisters born in east London. Like many others, in her life she moved along often searching for more, but never sure what that 'more' was. Jacqueline found what she was looking for in January 1995 when she found Jesus Christ and became a Christian. Since then her life has turned around in more ways than one.

It's hard to believe that Jacqueline did not like or write poetry before she began writing her first book in the Deep Calleth Unto Deep Series, in May 1997.

Her ministry is unique! She shares a message of healing, hope, and restoration as she encourages and challenges us to live purpose-filled lives. As a person Jacqueline is very 'real', open, honest and transparent. It is through this and her messages that many have opened the door to allow the Holy Spirit to work miraculously in their lives.

Jacqueline also runs her own training and development company, Training With Purpose, offering high quality training and development solutions to church and secular organisations alike. In addition to this busy schedule, she speaks at and organises conferences and workshops using her poems, experiences and books to take us on a healing journey.

As you peel back the pages of her books you will find warmth that is ever present as in Jacqueline herself. With all that's negative in life Jacqueline offers you something that's positive!

STAY IN TOUCH!

If this or any of the publications by Jacqueline Peart have blessed and encouraged you and you want to let her know please write to the address below:

United Kingdom:

PO Box 23606
London, England
E7 9TS

United States:

PO Box 220
Uniondale
New York
11553

Email:

Info@deepcallethuntodeep.com

Website:

www.deepcallethuntodeep.com
To hear from Jacqueline each week through her weekly inspirations:
Go to www.deepcallethuntodeep.com/inspirations.html

Other books in the Deep Calleth Unto Deep Series by the author:

Inspirations for Women… A Journey to Wholeness
In Search of Wholeness
Relationships
Images
Singleness

Deep Calleth Unto Deep

In Search of Wholeness

by Jacqueline Peart, Inspired by The Holy Spirit

'Jacqueline has written a book direct, heart-warming and powerfully inspiring. Yet simple enough for children to read, but definitely a book that every adult should digest.'

Bev Hendricks

Deep Calleth Unto Deep **In Search of Wholeness** is the first of a series of publications that have been developed to inspire and encourage those of you embarking on a journey to establish your self-esteem.

The author has used her own life experiences and thoughts to develop this new and moving account of self and esteem. So,

'...If lately you've begun to feel like your "perfect" world is falling apart, the things that seemed simple now seem like great quests, a gentle word now needs to be explained and you're questioning who you are and why you are, then read on my friend the Lord is about to move you on to be greater in Him.'

'And for those of you who like me six or seven years ago, thinks that everything is fine because you drive the right car, have a great job or business, house and all the rest of it, don't switch off or decide this book is not for you, because sometimes we can't see what's right in front us – the need for a richer more complete life, where externals are secondary and internals become primary.'

Deep Calleth Unto Deep

Relationships

by Jacqueline Peart, Inspired by The Holy Spirit

Deep Calleth Unto Deep, *Relationships* is the second in a series of publications that have been developed to inspire and encourage those of you seeking to establish and progress your self and esteem.

'Jacqueline A famous writer once said, '…if you want to know the condition of your community, listen to the music and read the works of the poets.' In this, Jacqueline Peart's latest book, she reflects the heart of the most touching aspects of our lives – RELATIONSHIPS. The book provides a provoking and real remedy to some of the difficulties we all experience in life.

Bev Hendricks, Editor

Relationships was hard for me to write and to publish because it challenged me and my integrity, it challenged my behaviour and most of all it challenged my faith and belief. You see relationships aren't always easy and they stir up old emotions and unresolved hurts. Read on and be blessed and be encouraged. As you read, consider where you are in your relationships…'

Jacqueline Peart, Author

Deep Calleth Unto Deep

IMAGES

by Jacqueline Peart, Inspired by The Holy Spirit

Deep Calleth Unto Deep, **IMAGES** is the third in a series of publications that have been developed to inspire and encourage those of you seeking to establish and progress your self and esteem.

The first thing God gave man was an image to be like Him – when you close your eyes and try to imagine God what picture do you see?

Images is a collection of poetic parables that vividly draws out the canvass of our spirit – the God in you and me.

Bev Hendricks

One of the most thought about and asked questions for the believer and the unbeliever must be, 'What does God look like?' I think I've found the answer. God looks like me and you, He can be found in every workplace, countryside, church, home and country. As you read **IMAGES** I believe you will agree with me if you don't already. So, be blessed and encouraged as I take you on my personal journey through poetry and thoughts.

Jacqueline Peart, Author

Deep Calleth Unto Deep

SINGLENESS

by Jacqueline Peart, Inspired by The Holy Spirit

Deep Calleth Unto Deep, **SINGLENESS** is the fourth in a series of publications, developed to help progress and establish your self and esteem. It is a collection of thoughts and poems that describe some of the feelings and thoughts you may encounter while you are single and unmarried or married and single...

At last
A book for the singles who have felt lonely, are asking why, are still waiting and have on occasions grown tired!

At last
A book which provides a timely reminder that you are not alone.

Bev Hendricks, Editor

'... if you're single, looking and waiting, I'm not going to say it's easy, I'm not going say it's unfair or even tell you to be patient, because no doubt many people have already told you that. What I will say is written in the pages of this book. As you read, **Deep Calleth Unto Deep, SINGLENESS** I pray you will keep **hoping** in Him and hold on because the vision is yet for an appointed time.

Jacqueline Peart, Author

Deep Calleth Unto Deep

Inspirations for Women... A Journey to Wholeness

by Jacqueline Peart, Inspired by The Holy Spirit

Jacqueline has written a book with truth and simplicity – love and warmth – and again and again sang the praises of Our Lord. This has, and will touch many lives...

To quote from her book:

'In 1997 I prayed a simple prayer: 'Lord, make me whole, make me be all you created me to be.' At that point my journey started. God began to show me how I compromised myself because of my need to be liked, loved and accepted. He began chiselling away at my character and personality, showing me my manmade strategies and showing me through His word, His strategies... I'm still allowing God to chip away at all the manmade and self-made masks and self-protection mechanisms that I have developed and it is truly a beautiful, yet at times uncomfortable and painful, process. Is it worth it? *Yes, every bit!*'

Jacqueline Peart